S. W. Tucker

Melodies of Life

A New Collection of Words and Music for the Choir, Congregation and Social Circle

S. W. Tucker

Melodies of Life

A New Collection of Words and Music for the Choir, Congregation and Social Circle

ISBN/EAN: 9783337296698

Printed in Europe, USA, Canada, Australia, Japan

Cover: Foto ©Thomas Meinert / pixelio.de

More available books at **www.hansebooks.com**

THE MELODIES OF LIFE.

A NEW COLLECTION OF

WORDS AND MUSIC

FOR THE

CHOIR, CONGREGATION,

AND

SOCIAL CIRCLE.

BY

S. W. TUCKER.

Author of various musical publications.

BOSTON:
COLBY AND RICH, PUBLISHERS,
BOSWORTH ST. (FORMERLY MONTGOMERY PL.),
1884.

PREFACE.

By the request of friends we bring before the lovers of song another collection of words and music in which are combined "Golden Melodies" and "Spiritual Echoes," with the addition of many new pieces never before published, making in all a book of one hundred and twenty pages. We have tried to comply with the wishes of others by writing easy and pleasing melodies, and in selecting such words as will be acceptable to mortals and find a response with the angels who may join us in the singing of them.

S. W. TUCKER.

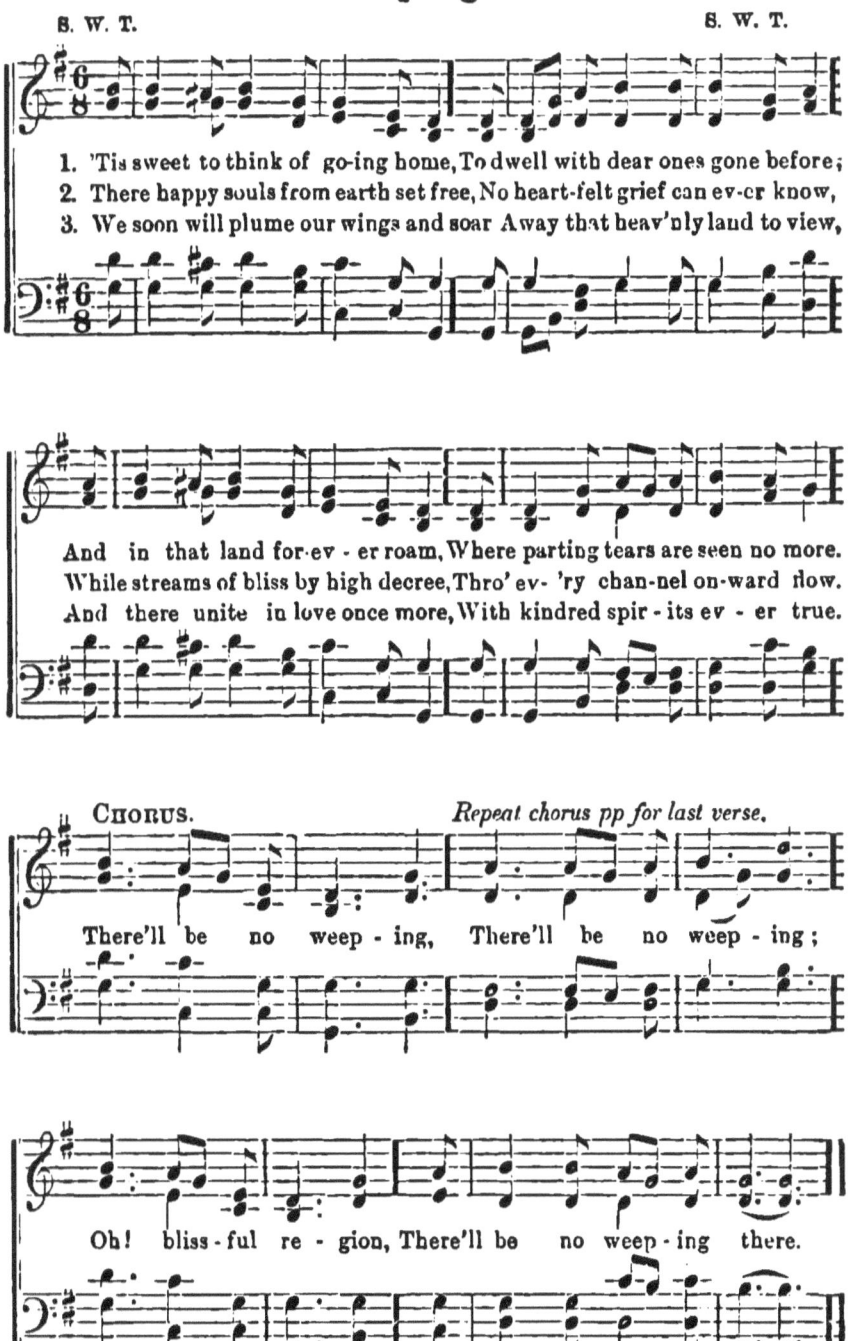

WE SHALL MEET ON THE BRIGHT CELESTIAL SHORE.

Words and Music by S. W. TUCKER.

1. We shall meet beyond the ri-ver, All the loved ones gone before;
2. We shall meet in that bright arbor, Where an-gel-ic lays are heard;

We shall meet no more to sever, On the bright cel-es-tial shore.
There the weary find a har-bor, And no heart with grief is stirr'd.

CHORUS.

Then we'll meet, ne'er to part, When the boatman takes us o'er;
ne'er to part, ne'er to part,

We shall meet a-gain the pure in heart, On the bright ce-les-tial shore.

3. We shall meet beyond the billows,
   Where no storm can o'er us beat,
   And we'll rest on downy pillows,
   Such as none but angels keep.

4. We shall meet beyond the river,
   And partake of the repast,
   That the kind immortal giver,
   Will prepare for us at last.

They'll Welcome us Home.   7

S. W. T.   S. W. T.

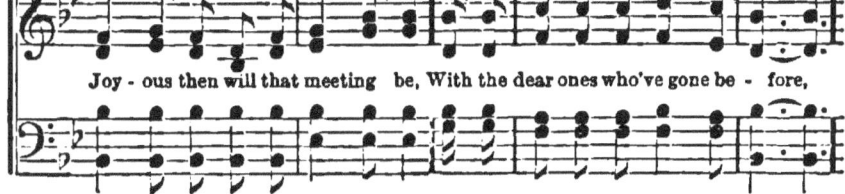

2
We're moving down the stream of time,
   To the port where no surges foam,
We'll anchor in a fairer clime,
   And angels will welcome us home.
      Joyous then, &c.

3
A summons from the courts above,
   To us mortals ere long will come;
And we'll respond in tones of love,
   For angels will welcome us home.
      Joyous then, &c.

Looking Beyond.

Words by Rev. A. J. LOCKHART.   S. W. TUCKER.

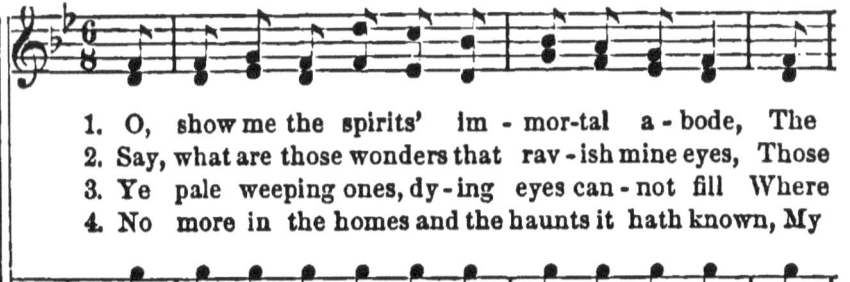

1. O, show me the spirits' im-mor-tal a-bode, The
2. Say, what are those wonders that rav-ish mine eyes, Those
3. Ye pale weeping ones, dy-ing eyes can-not fill Where
4. No more in the homes and the haunts it hath known, My

homes of the beauti-ful there; For the place of a mortal at
phantoms of flowers and streams That dart on the gaze of my
sunbeams of glo-ry have shone; The hand of the earth-ly is
spir-it delighteth to be, I am launching my boat in the

home with his God, The hope of the dy-ing pre - pare.
soul from the skies; Then melt in a glo-ry of dreams.
los-ing its thrill; Earth's music its mel-low-est tone.
shadows a-lone; On the shores of a fath-om-less sea.

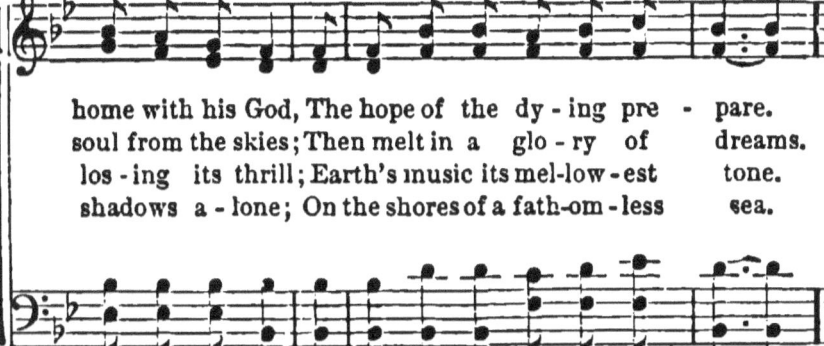

Not Yet.

Words by Mrs. M. J. WENTWORTH. S. W. TUCKER.

1. Not yet can I sing like the wild bird, Whose heart is with summer at-tune:
When the perfume of li-lacs and ros-es, Make fragrant the breezes of June:
For birds on-ly sing in their glad-ness At morn, or 'mid splendor of day.
But their notes have an ech-o of sad-ness, 'Neath evening's pavilion of gray.

2
Not yet can I chant like the river,
  That murmurs along in its glee;
While telling to meadow and wildwood,
  A tale of the beautiful sea.
Not yet can I speak in a language,
  With musical notes in each tone;
For over my spirit too rudely
  The tempests of sorrow have blown.

3
But when I awake in the morning
  And soar in the summer land's June,
O then I will sing for you darling,
  With harpchords and heaven attune;
'Till then I must sing for you darling,
  Like birds at the close of the day;
While I wait for the beautiful morning,
  Whose dawn-light is tinging the gray.

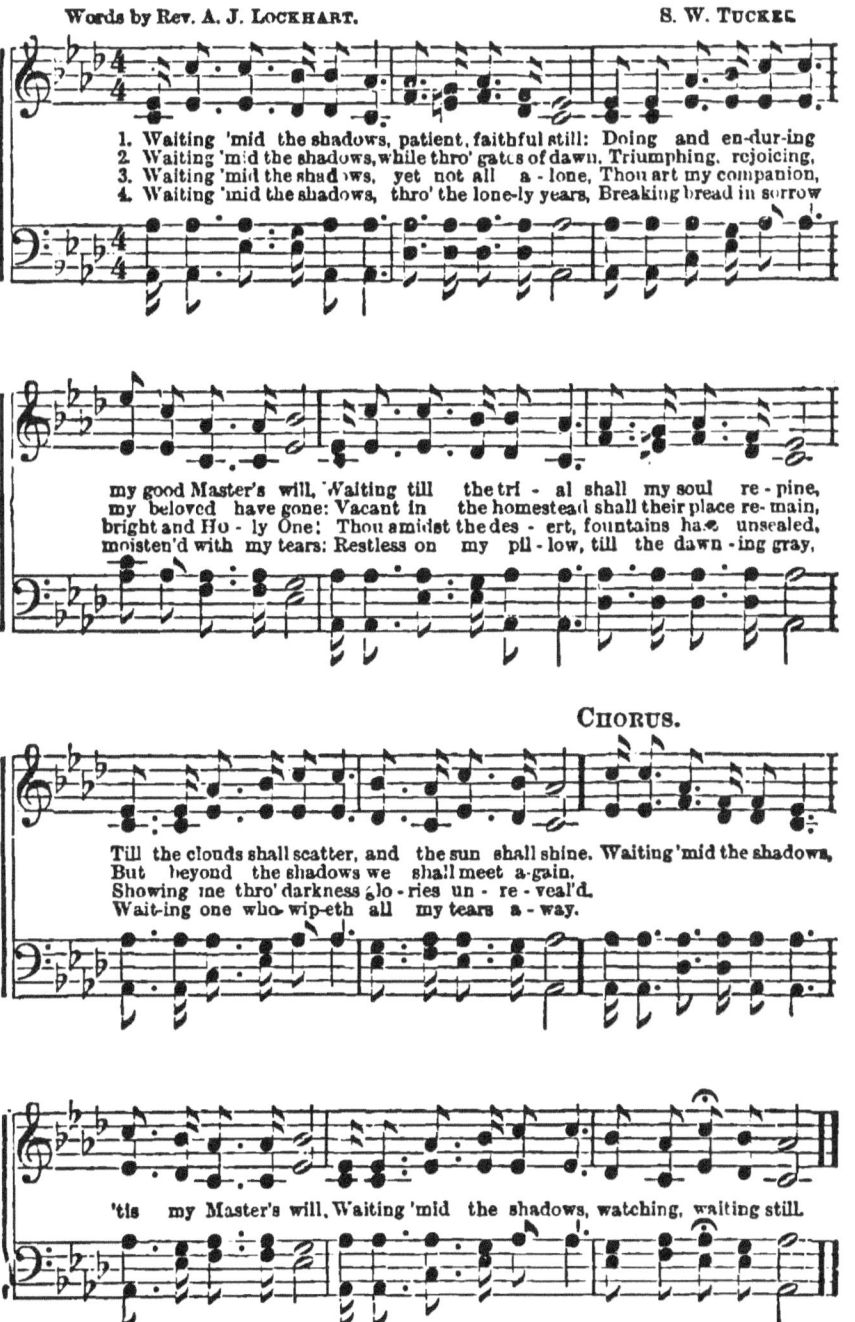

Sweet Hour of Prayer.

Words by Rev. W. W. WALFORD, 1849.
S. W. TUCKER.

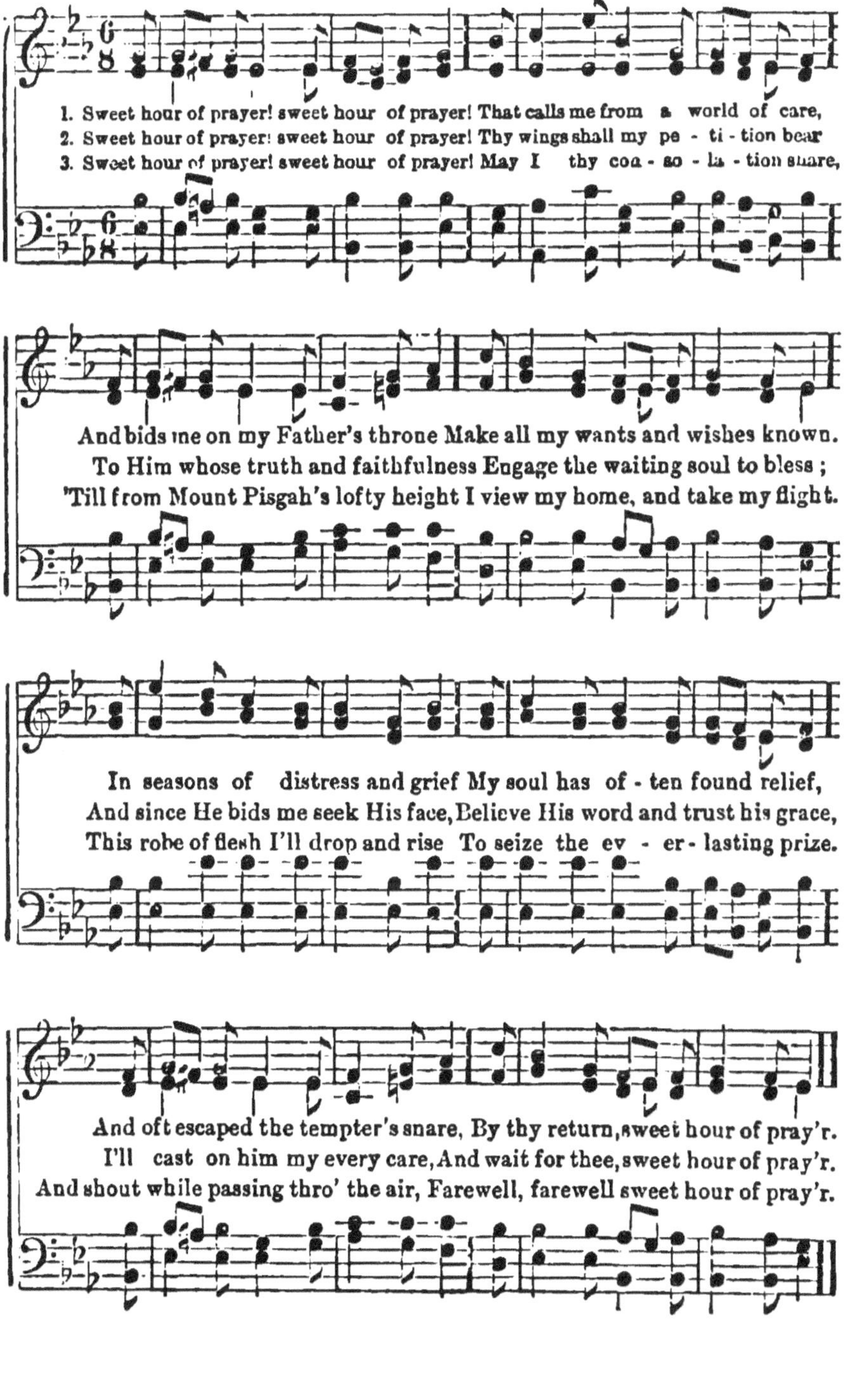

1. Sweet hour of prayer! sweet hour of prayer! That calls me from a world of care,
2. Sweet hour of prayer! sweet hour of prayer! Thy wings shall my petition bear
3. Sweet hour of prayer! sweet hour of prayer! May I thy consolation share,

And bids me on my Father's throne Make all my wants and wishes known.
To Him whose truth and faithfulness Engage the waiting soul to bless;
'Till from Mount Pisgah's lofty height I view my home, and take my flight.

In seasons of distress and grief My soul has often found relief,
And since He bids me seek His face, Believe His word and trust his grace,
This robe of flesh I'll drop and rise To seize the ever-lasting prize.

And oft escaped the tempter's snare, By thy return, sweet hour of pray'r.
I'll cast on him my every care, And wait for thee, sweet hour of pray'r.
And shout while passing thro' the air, Farewell, farewell sweet hour of pray'r.

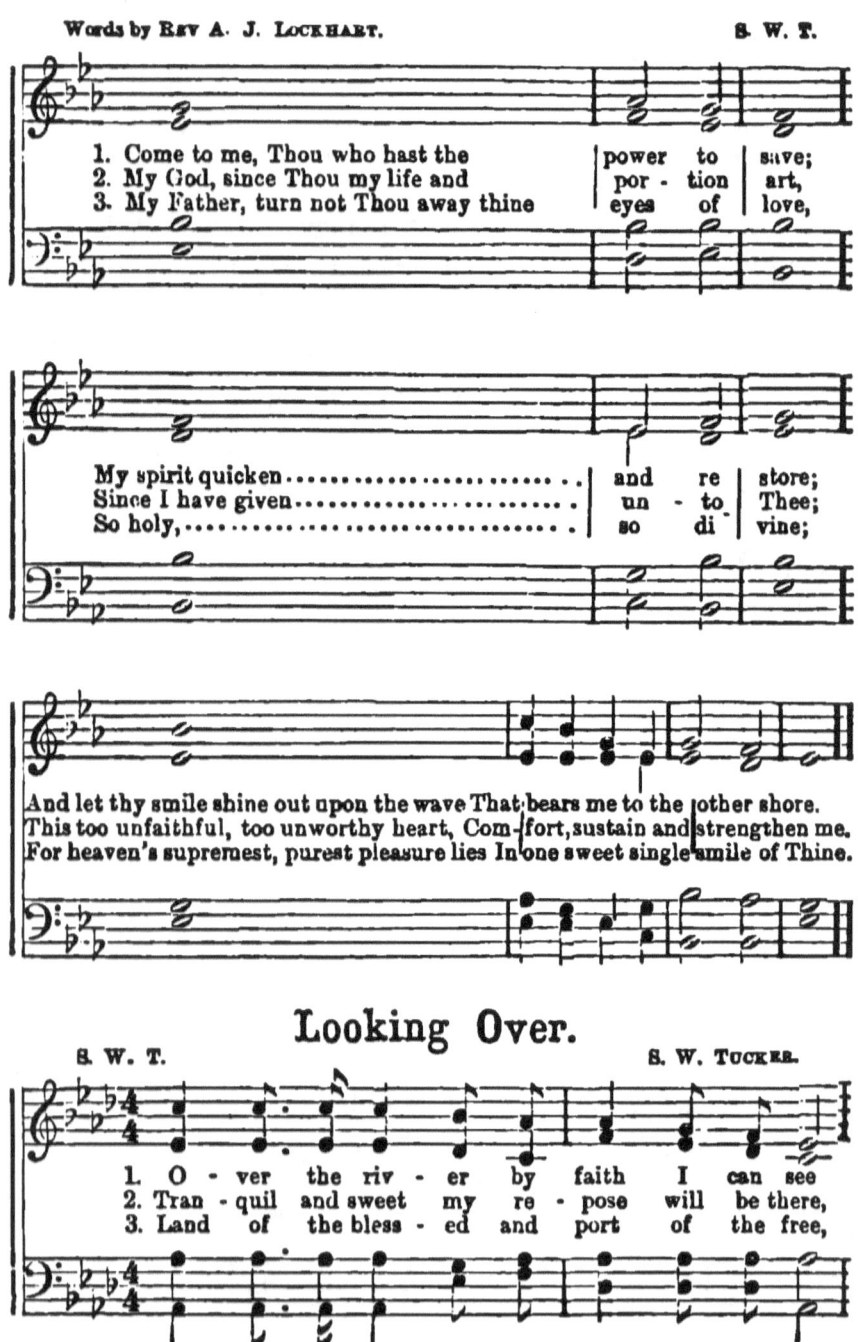

Looking Over. Concluded. 19

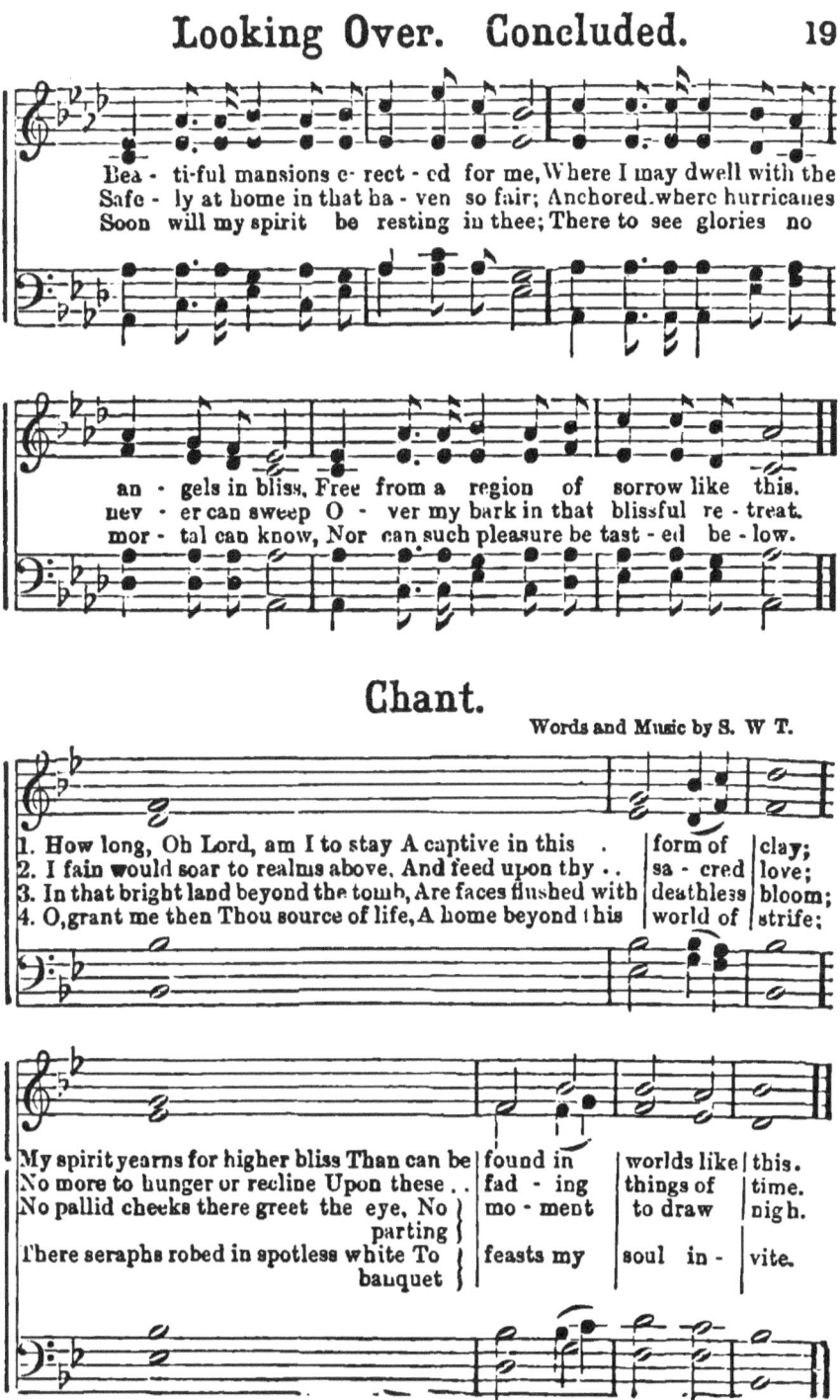

Bea - ti-ful mansions e- rect - ed for me, Where I may dwell with the an - gels in bliss, Free from a region of sorrow like this.
Safe - ly at home in that ha - ven so fair; Anchored.where hurricanes nev - er can sweep O - ver my bark in that blissful re - treat.
Soon will my spirit be resting in thee; There to see glories no mor - tal can know, Nor can such pleasure be tast - ed be - low.

Chant.

Words and Music by S. W T.

1. How long, Oh Lord, am I to stay A captive in this . . | form of	clay;
2. I fain would soar to realms above, And feed upon thy . . | sa - cred	love;
3. In that bright land beyond the tomb, Are faces flushed with | deathless	bloom;
4. O, grant me then Thou source of life, A home beyond this | world of	strife;

My spirit yearns for higher bliss Than can be | found in	worlds like | this.
No more to hunger or recline Upon these . . | fad - ing	things of | time.
No pallid cheeks there greet the eye, No) | mo - ment	to draw | nigh.
parting)		
There seraphs robed in spotless white To (| feasts my	soul in - | vite.
banquet)		

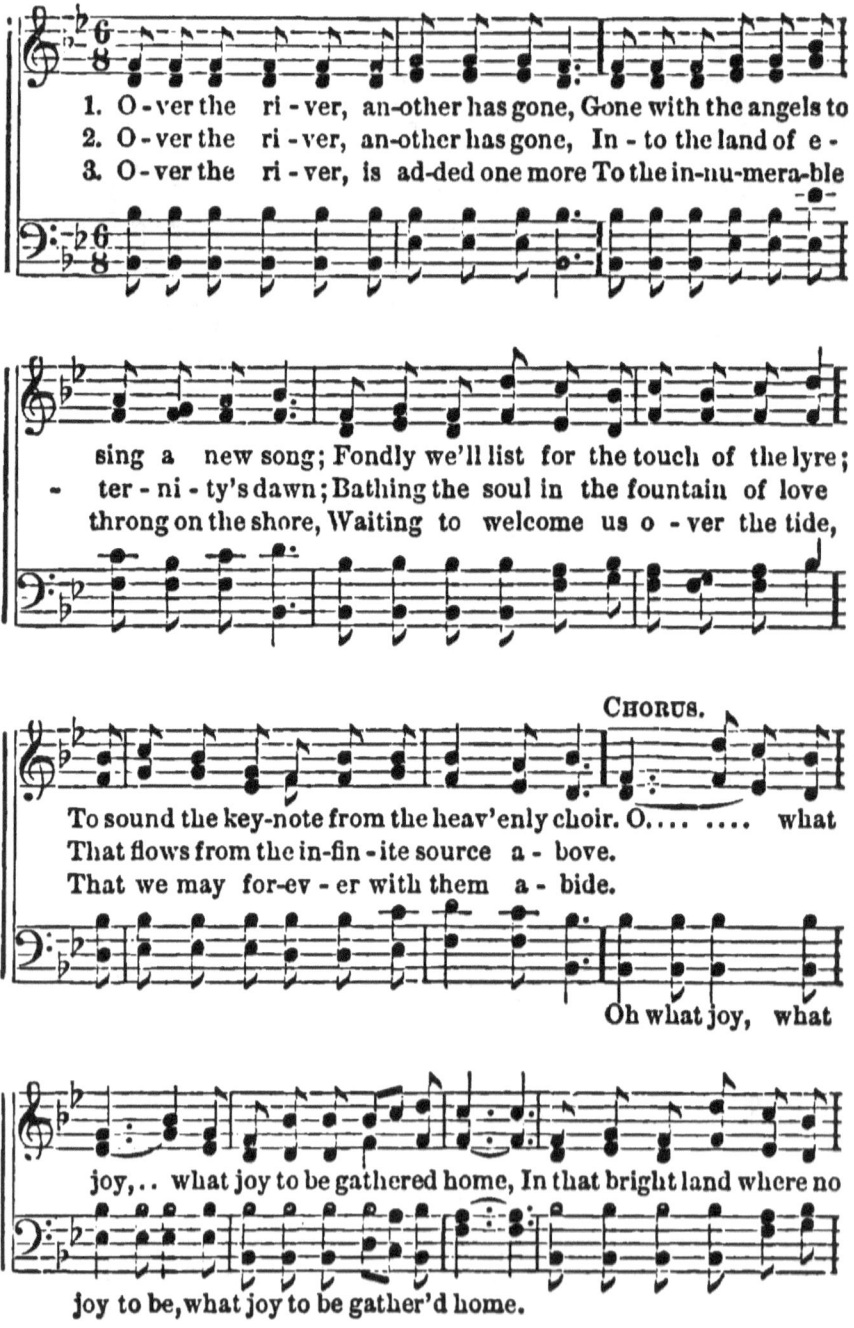

Gathered Home.—Concluded.

Moving Homeward.

S. W. T. S. W. Tucker.

1. We're moving down the stream of time, Whose waters flow by law di-vine;
2. There mountains clad in vernal hue, A-rise to meet the spirit's view,

Thro' chan - nels fash - ion'd not .... with hands, We're
As we .... draw near the gold - en stand, To

Thro' channels fashion'd not with hands, We're borne away to fairer lands,
As we draw near the golden strand, To make complete our broken band,

borne a - way .... to fair - er lands.
make com - plete .... our brok - en band.

We're borne a - way to fair - er lands.
To make com - plete our brok - en band.

3. How sweet to think of going home,
To toss no more on life's rough foam;
But ever glide o'er seas of bliss,
That find no place in worlds like this.

# Angel Visitants.

Words and Music by S. W. TUCKER.

1. From the land of light and glory, Come the an-gel lov'd ones now,
2. Must these angel voices leave me, And the strains die on my ear,
3. Tho' I often here find pleasure, Mingled with these hopes and fears,

Bringing balms of rarest beauty, And they place them on my brow.
Father, grant that this may not be, While on earth I lin-ger here.
Yet my fond, my dearest treasure, Lies beyond this vale of tears.

Sweeter than the rose of morning, Is the o-dor on the air;
Could I go to heaven with them, All the dear ones there to meet,
Soon I'll bid farewell to sorrow, And resign this earthly cot,

Ris-ing from these now adorning Flow'rs upon my silk-en hair.
Then my heart no more would sadden, And my joy would be complete.
The ce-les-tial band to follow, Where the lily fad-eth not.

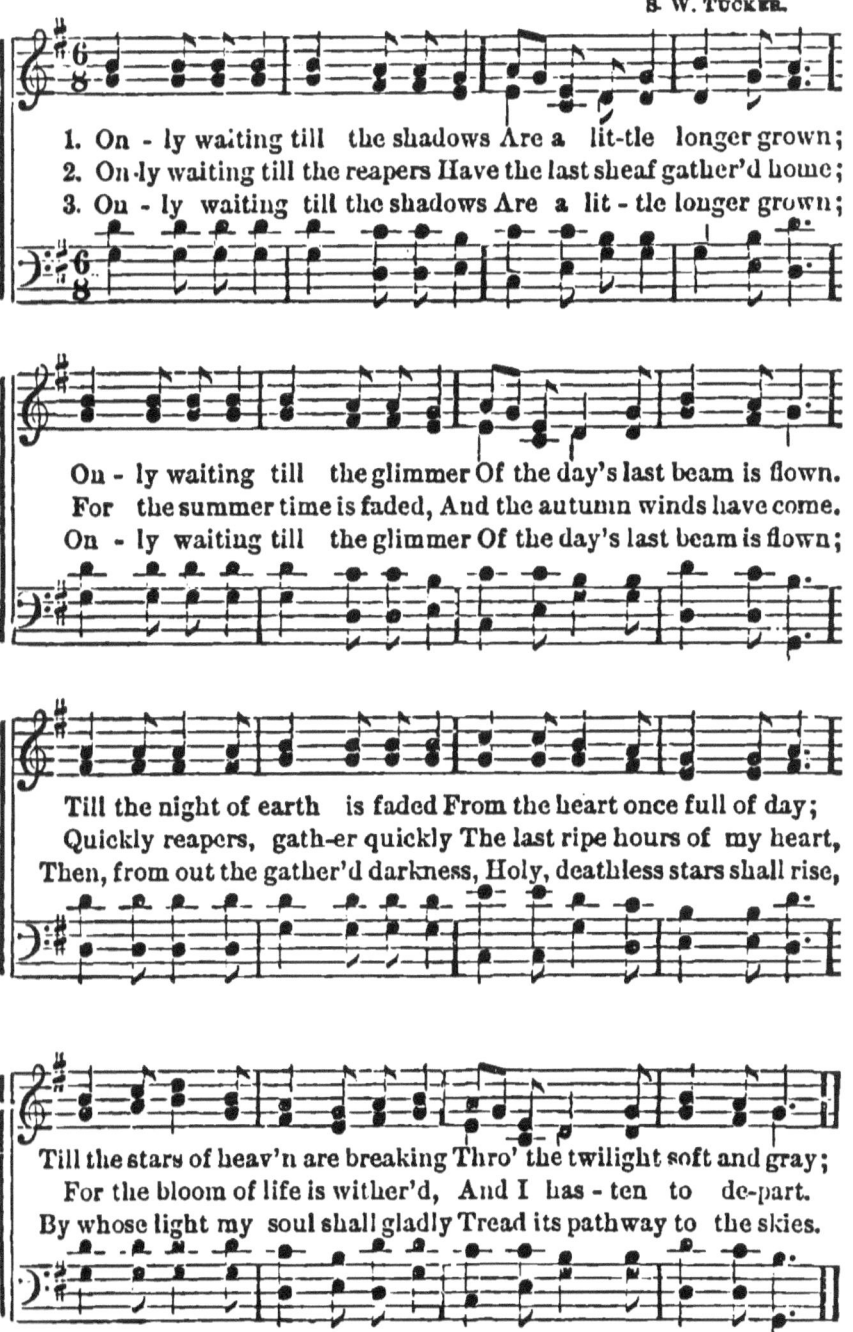

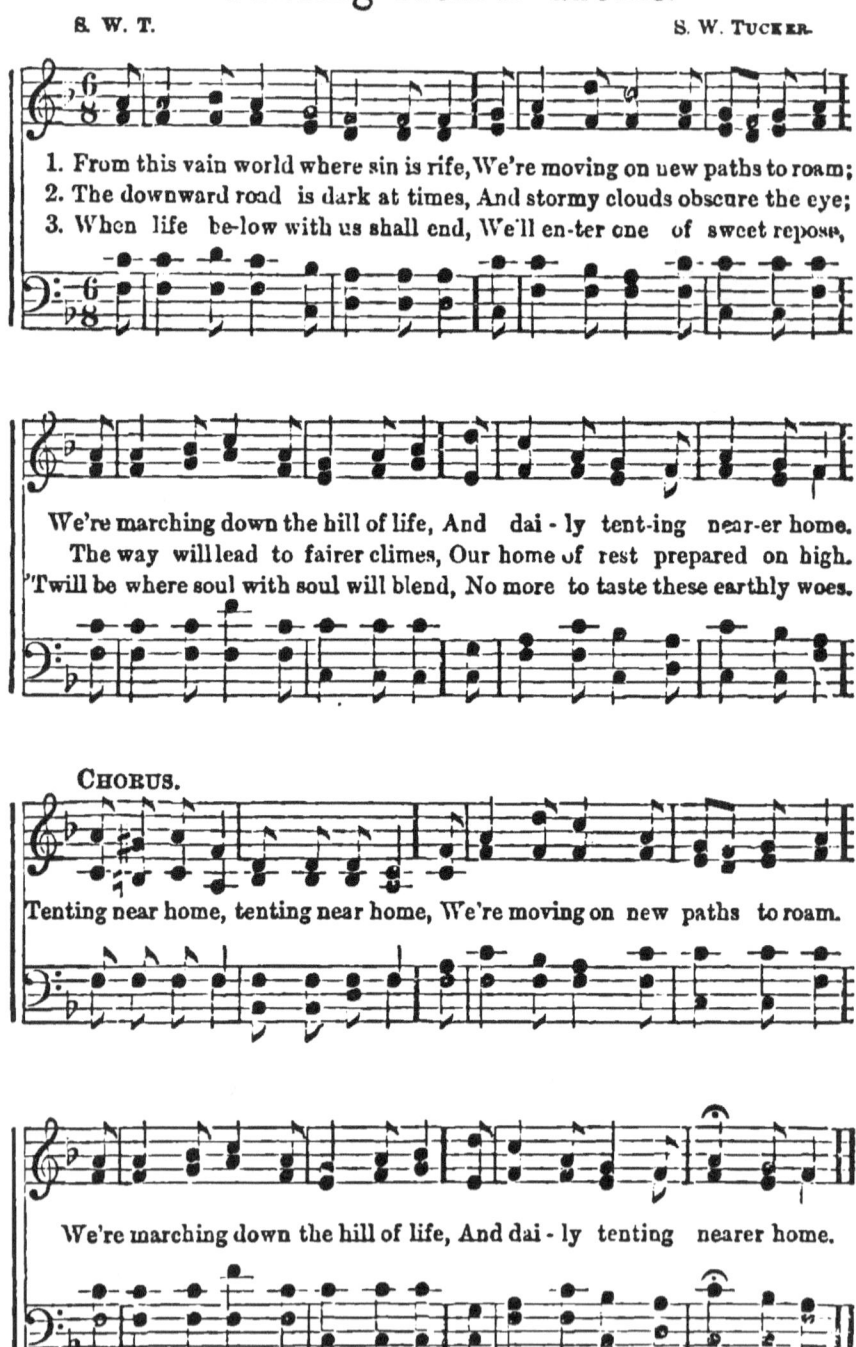

Evergreen Shore.

Words and Music by S. W. TUCKER.
From "Spiritual Harp," by per.

1. This world of strife is not our home, We're bound for the evergreen shore,
2. They beckon on our way along, We press for the evergreen shore;
3. There fadeless garlands ever bloom, In paths on the evergreen shore;

That land of beauty where loved one have gone, Our loved ones forever more.
We soon shall enter that heavenly throng, Where parting shall be no more.
Where pain and sickness, bereavement and gloom, Shall mar our repose no more.

CHORUS.

Rest, rest, forever at home, Where pain and distress shall be o'er; We yearn to be free in those realms to roam, Our home on the evergreen shore.

Home of Rest.—Concluded.

We are go-ing o'er the river, To our home of rest so free,
We will go and share it ever, That sweet rest for you and me.

Gone Before. C. M.

Words and Music by S. W. Tucker.

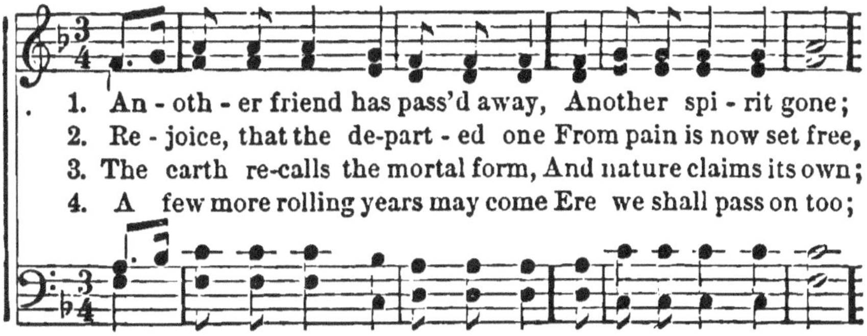

1. An - oth - er friend has pass'd away, Another spi - rit gone;
2. Re - joice, that the de-part - ed one From pain is now set free,
3. The earth re-calls the mortal form, And nature claims its own;
4. A few more rolling years may come Ere we shall pass on too;

Freed from its form of mould'ring clay, To dwell in peace at home.
And life im mor - tal is begun Where sorrow ne'er can be.
The soul is shelter'd from the storm, That o'er it oft hath blown.
And hear the joyful welcome home, That heav'nly land to view.

Beautiful City.

S. W. T.
S. W. Tucker.

1. There's a beau-ti-ful ci-ty just o-ver the way,
2. We may hear of its pleas-ures and fos-ter-ing care;
3. To that ci-ty of ref-uge we'll soon take our flight,

Whose mansions im-mor-tal shall nev-er de-cay;
But bet-ter, far bet-ter 'twill be to be there,
With an-gels to dwell in trans-port-ed de-light;

It was founded and reared by the wisdom of Him,
Where the love of the Fa-ther for-ev-er will be,
Where the storm and the tem-pests no more can dis-turb,

Who cares for the wea-ry and gath-ers them in.
Displayed in its full-ness for you and for me.
Our rest and re-pose in that bliss-ful a-bode.

Beautiful City.—Concluded.

CHORUS.

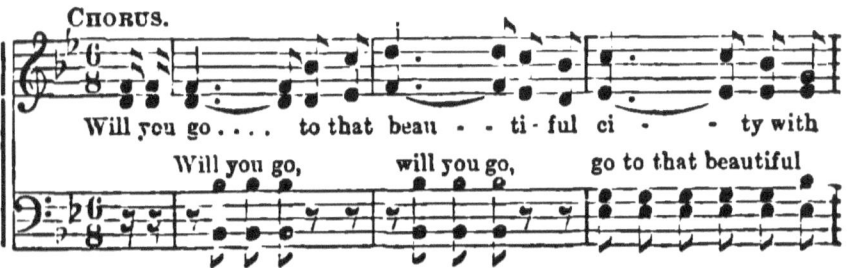

Will you go.... to that beau-ti-ful ci-ty with
Will you go, will you go, go to that beautiful

me,............ Whose man-sions im-mor-tal shall
ci-ty with me,

never decay, Will you go to that beau-ti-ful ci-ty with me.

We welcome them here.

Words and Music by S. W. TUCKER.

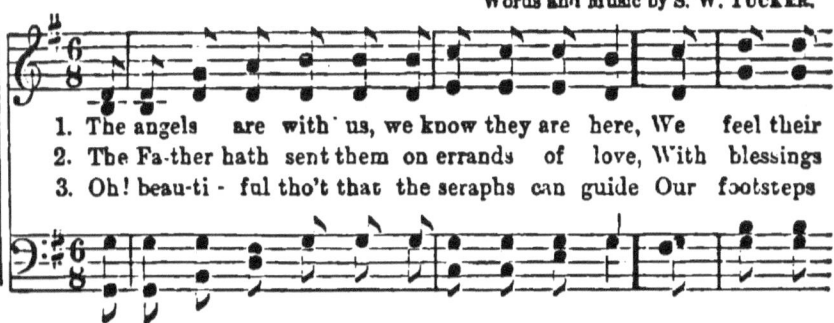

1. The angels are with us, we know they are here, We feel their
2. The Father hath sent them on errands of love, With blessings
3. Oh! beau-ti-ful tho't that the seraphs can guide Our footsteps

A little while longer.

Voices from the Better Land. 37

Words by Rev. A. J. LOCKHART. S. W. T.

1. Sometimes to earth may the brightness come Thro' azure deeps from their star-ry home; And in our ears may their cho-rus swell; Sweet as the murmur of o-cean's shell; We hear the music of trembling strings, And feel the pul-sing of view-less wings.

2. When 'mid the toil and the heat of day, The feet grow weary a-long the way, The hea-vy bur-den of grief and care; Is sometimes more than the heart can bear. We hear their whispers at ev-en-tide, That hush our griefs and our cares sub-side.

3. When in the sky are the stars so bright, And o'er the earth comes the balm-y night; When gen-tle sleep on the wea-ried eye, Like bead-ed dew on the flow'rs may lie; They come to us, with e-lys-ian dreams Of pear-ly gates and the liv-ing streams.

4. Is there a heart that doth weep and bleed, Is there a soul that doth meek-ly plead; Lo! one with ten-der-est smile shall come Out thro' the gate of her angel home; Then peace, sweet peace shall that soul re-store, And th' heart shall sor-row and bleed no more.

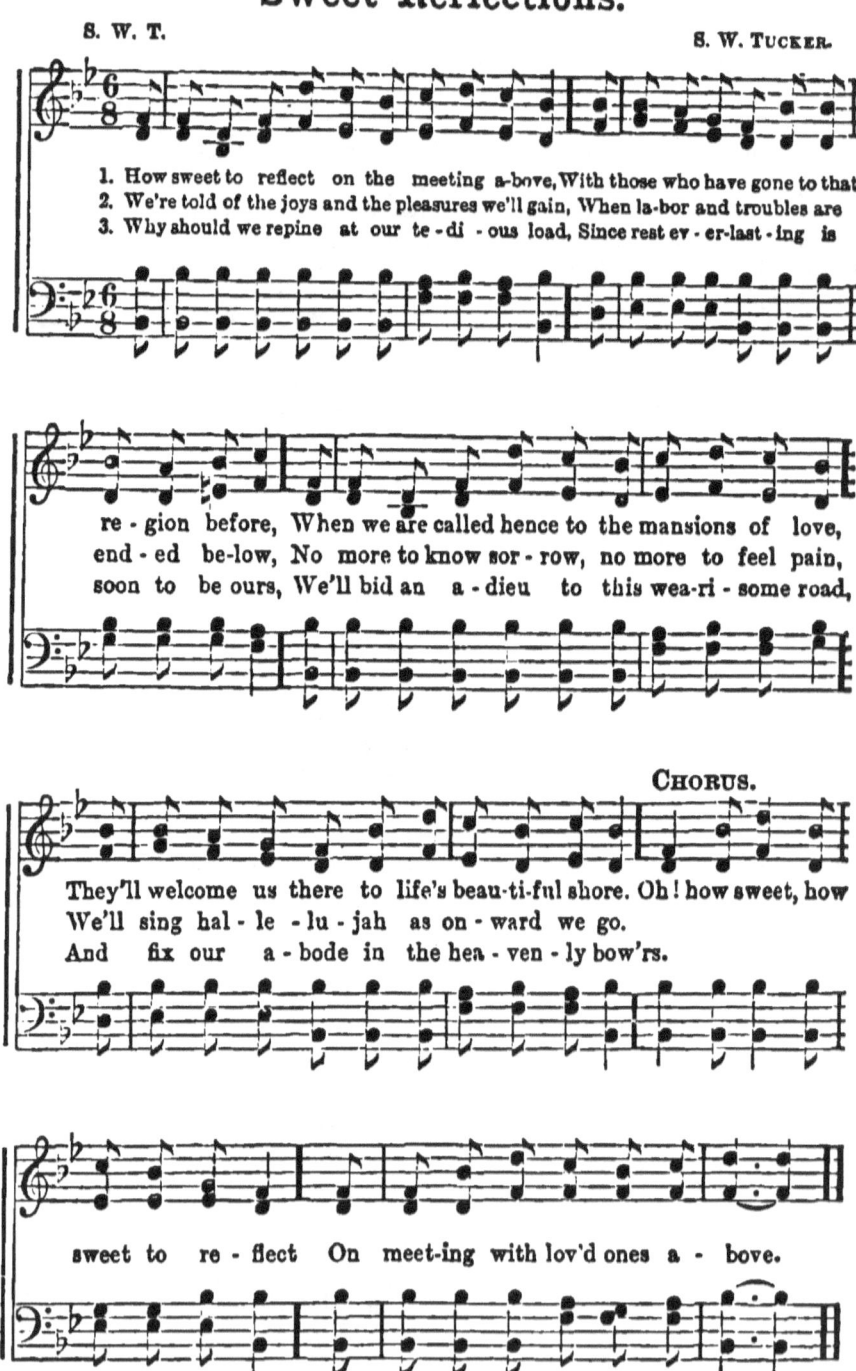

Sweet Reflections.—Concluded.

When we are called hence to life's beau-ti-ful shore;

They'll wel-come us there to the man-sions of love.

By-and-By. (Hymn Chant.)

Words by Mrs. M. J. WENTWORTH.   S. W. T.

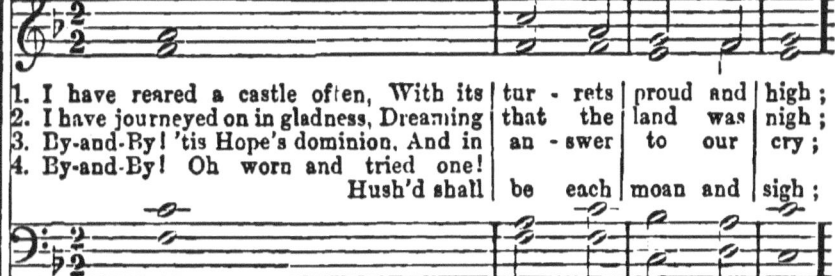

1. I have reared a castle often, With its | tur - rets | proud and | high ;
2. I have journeyed on in gladness, Dreaming | that the | land was | nigh ;
3. By-and-By! 'tis Hope's dominion, And in | an - swer | to our | cry ;
4. By-and-By! Oh worn and tried one! Hush'd shall | be each | moan and | sigh ;

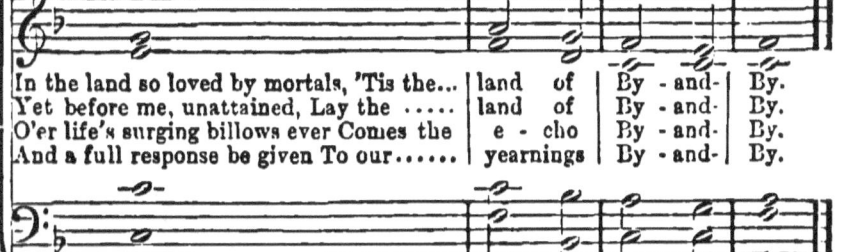

In the land so loved by mortals, 'Tis the... | land of | By - and- | By.
Yet before me, unattained, Lay the ..... | land of | By - and- | By.
O'er life's surging billows ever Comes the | e - cho | By - and- | By.
And a full response be given To our...... | yearnings | By - and- | By.

Angel Friends.

S. W. TUCKER.

1. Floating on the breath of evening, Breathing in the morning pray'r,
2. We forget, while list'ning to them, All the sorrows we have known,
3. Soothing with their magic whispers, Calming all our wildest fear
4. Bless you, angel friends, oh, never Leave us lonely on the way!

Hear we oft the tender voices That once made our world so fair.
And upon the troubles present, Faith's pure shining light is thrown.
Thus they bring us sweet submission; Peace for sorrow, smiles for tears.
For your gentle teachings ever Meekly may we watch and pray.

Trust in God.

Words by Mrs. M. J. WENTWORTH.   S. W. TUCKER.

1. Once when morning's rosy light, Ting'd with gold the eastern hill,
2. Trust thro' sorrow, pain and doubt, May thy heart with anguish fill,
3. Years have flown since that spring-morn, Years with winter's storm and chill,
4. And by this sweet lesson taught, Oft my wayward heart I still,

Sang sweet voices thro' my pray'r, Trust in God and fear no ill.
For His hand shall guide thee on, Trust in God and fear no ill.
Yet the voice sings in my heart, Trust in God and fear no ill.
Doubts dispel and fears depart, When I trust, and fear no ill.

42. Sweet Meeting There.

Words and Music by S. W. Tucker.

1. We soon from this clay shall be free, To dwell in a region most fair;
2. There cities for-ever shall stand, Nor can they know death or decay;
3. That world is yet glowing with love, Its charms are alluring us there;

Where all our de-part-ed we'll see, And sweet will the meeting be there.
Since life in that beau-ti-ful land, Can nev-er be taken a-way.
The angels now call us a-bove, Our freedom from earth to declare.

CHORUS.

How sweet.... how sweet, how sweet will the meeting be there,
how sweet, how sweet,

With all our de-parted now free, How sweet will the meeting be there.

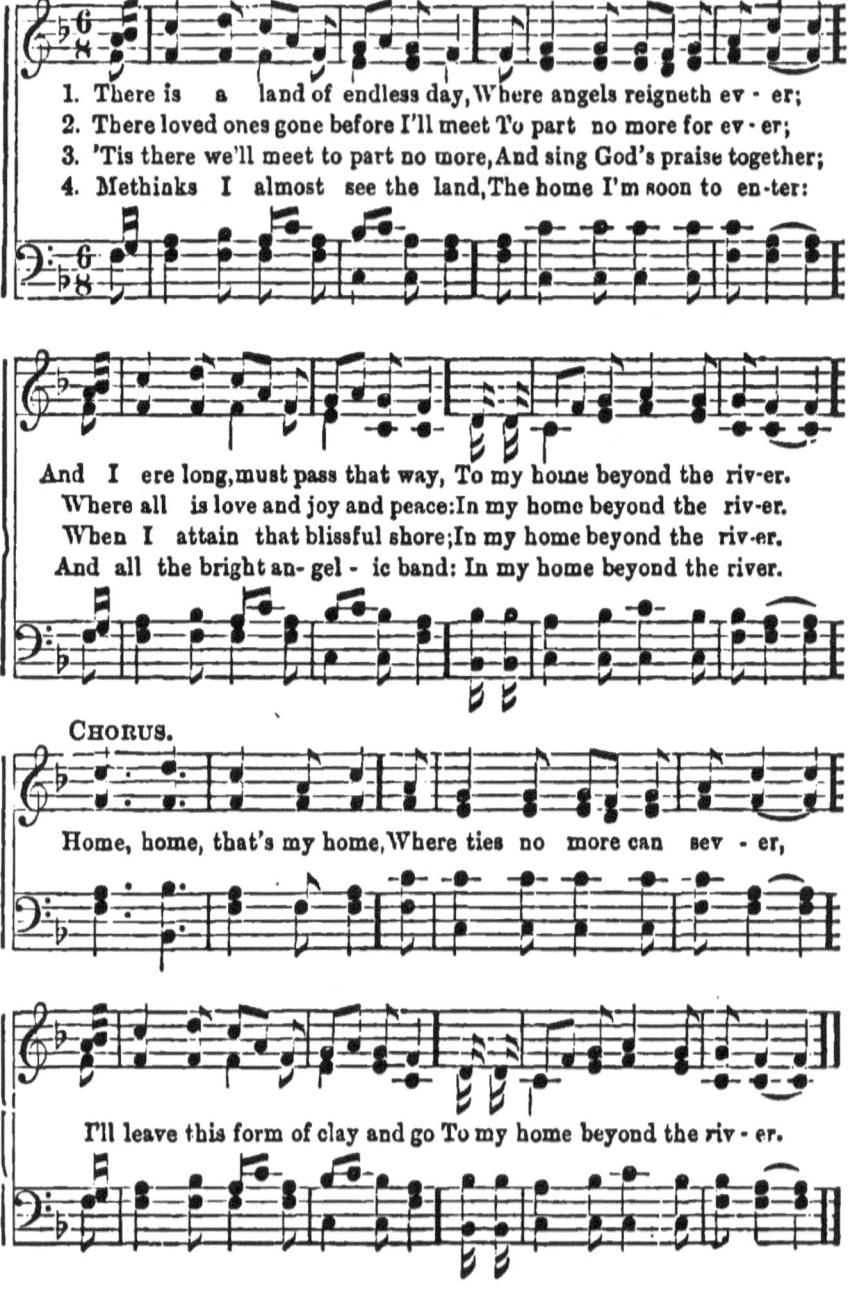

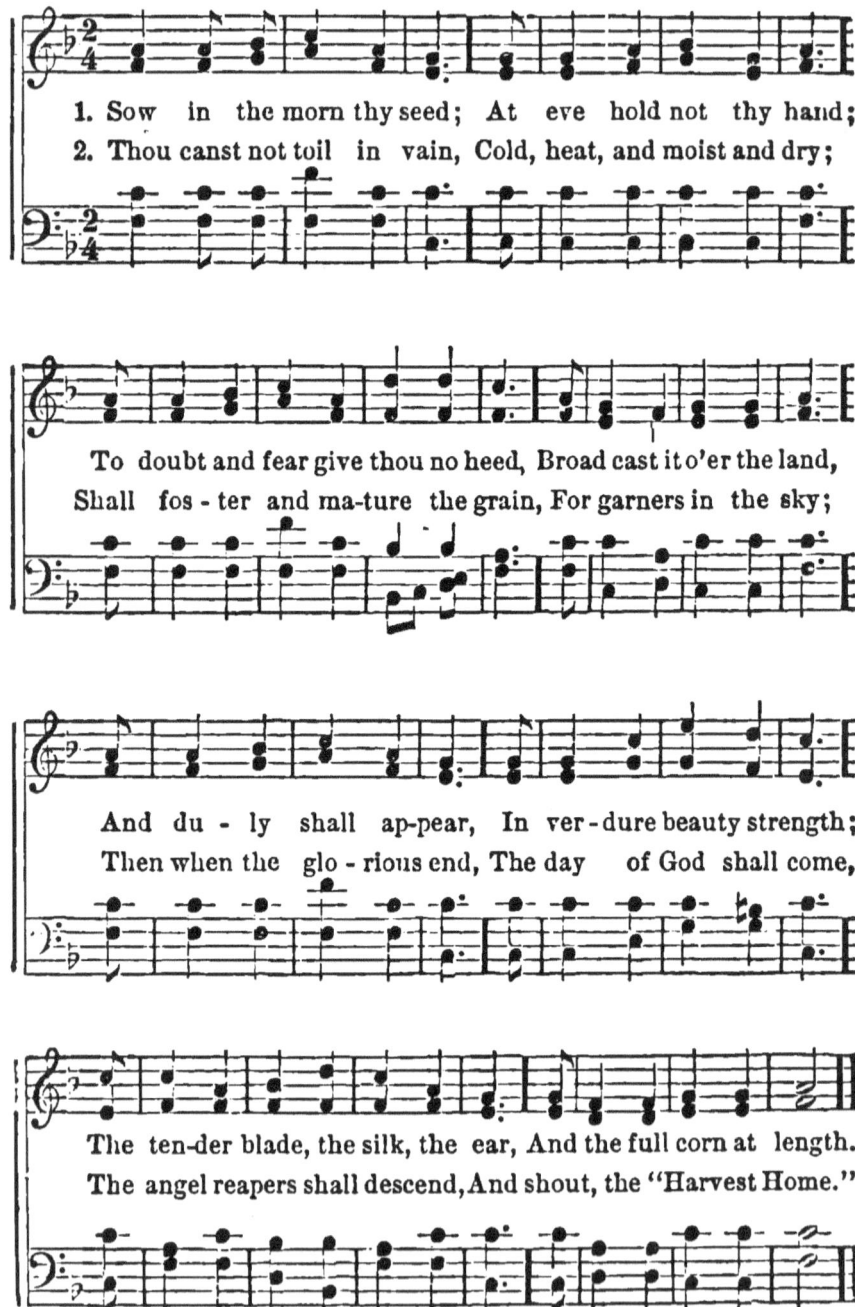

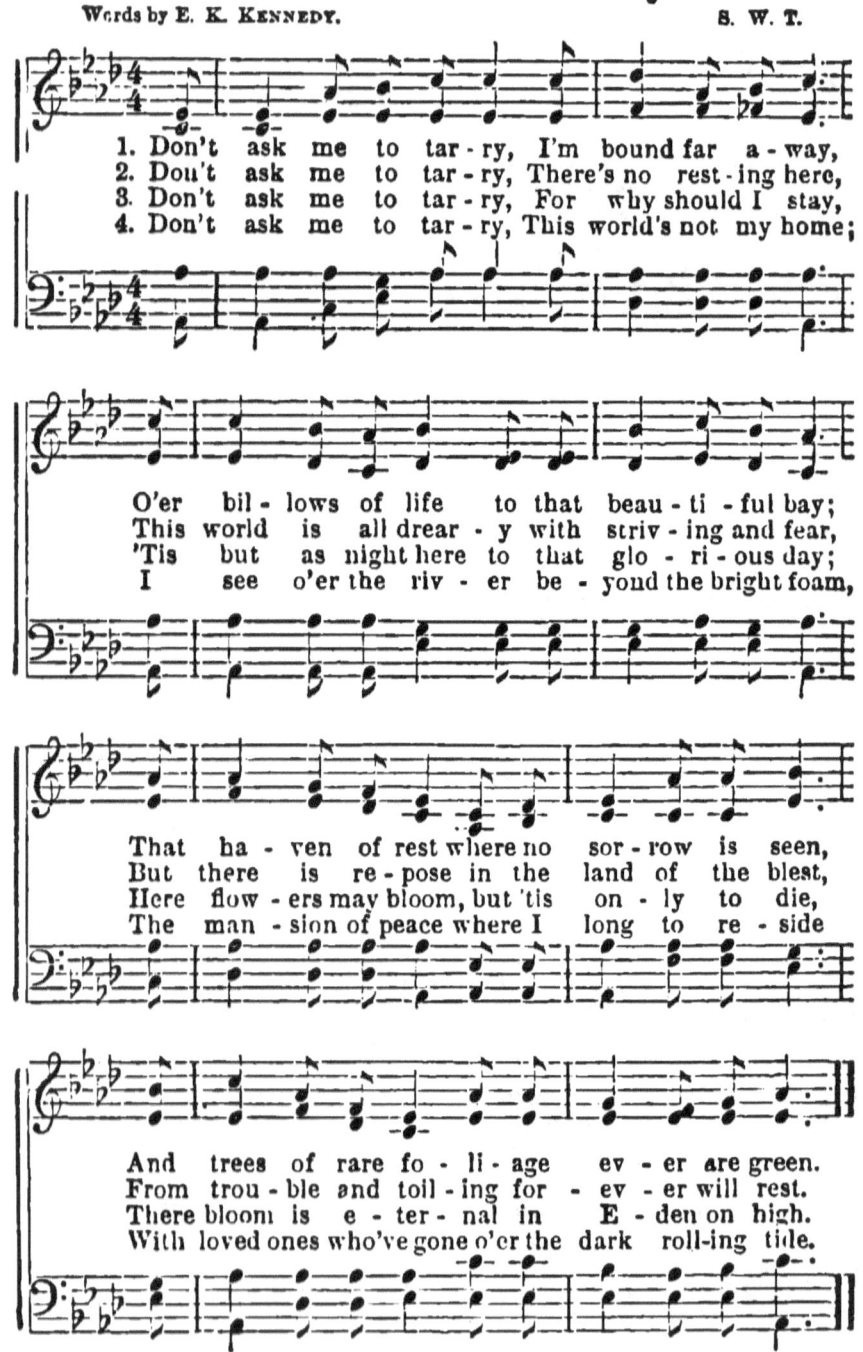

Over the River I'm going.

1 O-ver the riv-er I'm go-ing, My work is most end-ed be-low,
2 O-ver the riv-er I'm go-ing, My beau-ti-ful mansion to see,
3. O-ver the riv-er I'm go-ing, To meet the de-part-ed of yore,

Soon I'll remove to my dwelling, Where pleasures e-ter-nal-ly flow;
Ask me no long-er to tar-ry, For loved ones are waiting for me;
Meet in that re-gion of glo-ry, Where ties can be broken no more;

CHORUS.

Sweetly the bands are now playing, My sorrow on earth to dis-pel,

While a few moments I'm waiting, To go with the an-gels to dwell.

We're journeying on to-day.

1. We're jour-ney-ing on to-day, Our heav-en-ly home to see;
2. We're jour-ney-ing on to-day, To meet on the gold-en shore
3. We're jour-ney-ing on to-day, Bound o-ver the crys-tal sea,

Where zeph-yrs ce-les-tial play A-round o'er the ver-dant lea.
The loved ones who've gone that way, And crossed o'er the stream be-fore.
Where storms nev-er-more have sway, And peace-ful our rest will be.

REFRAIN.

We're journey-ing on, journeying on Our heaven-ly home to see,
Where zeph-yrs ce-les-tial play, A-round o'er the ver-dant lea.

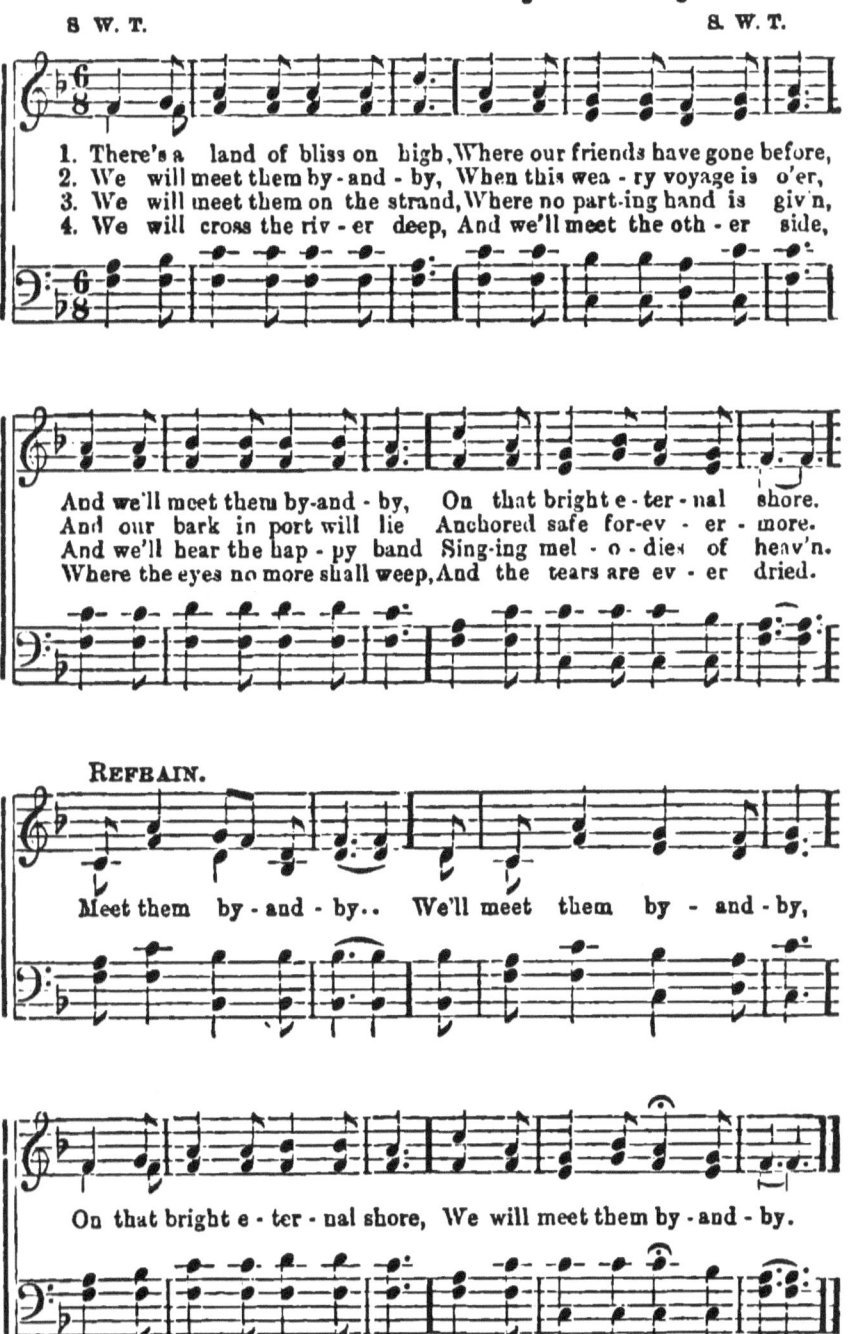

Flowers in heaven.

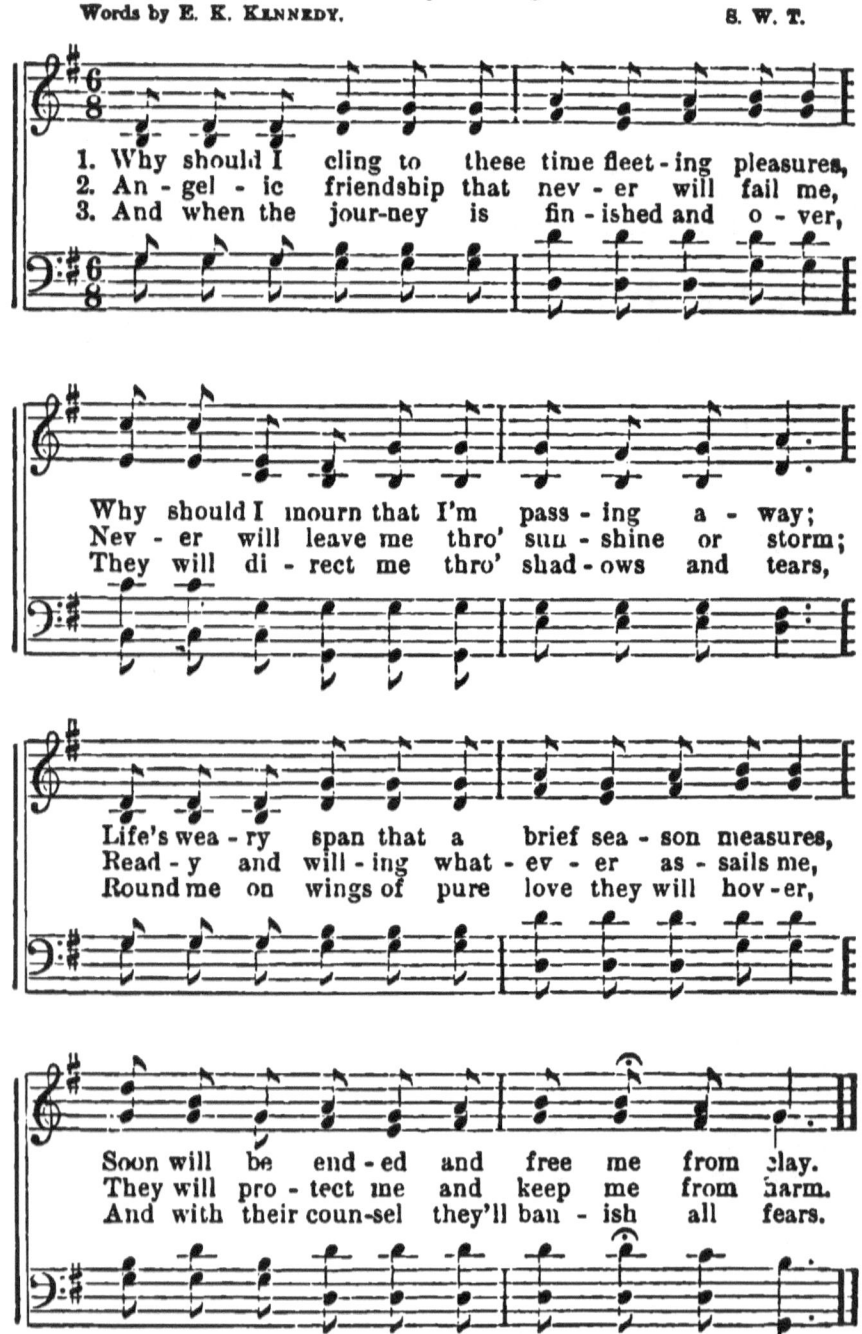

Where shadows fall no more.

S. W. T. S. W. T.

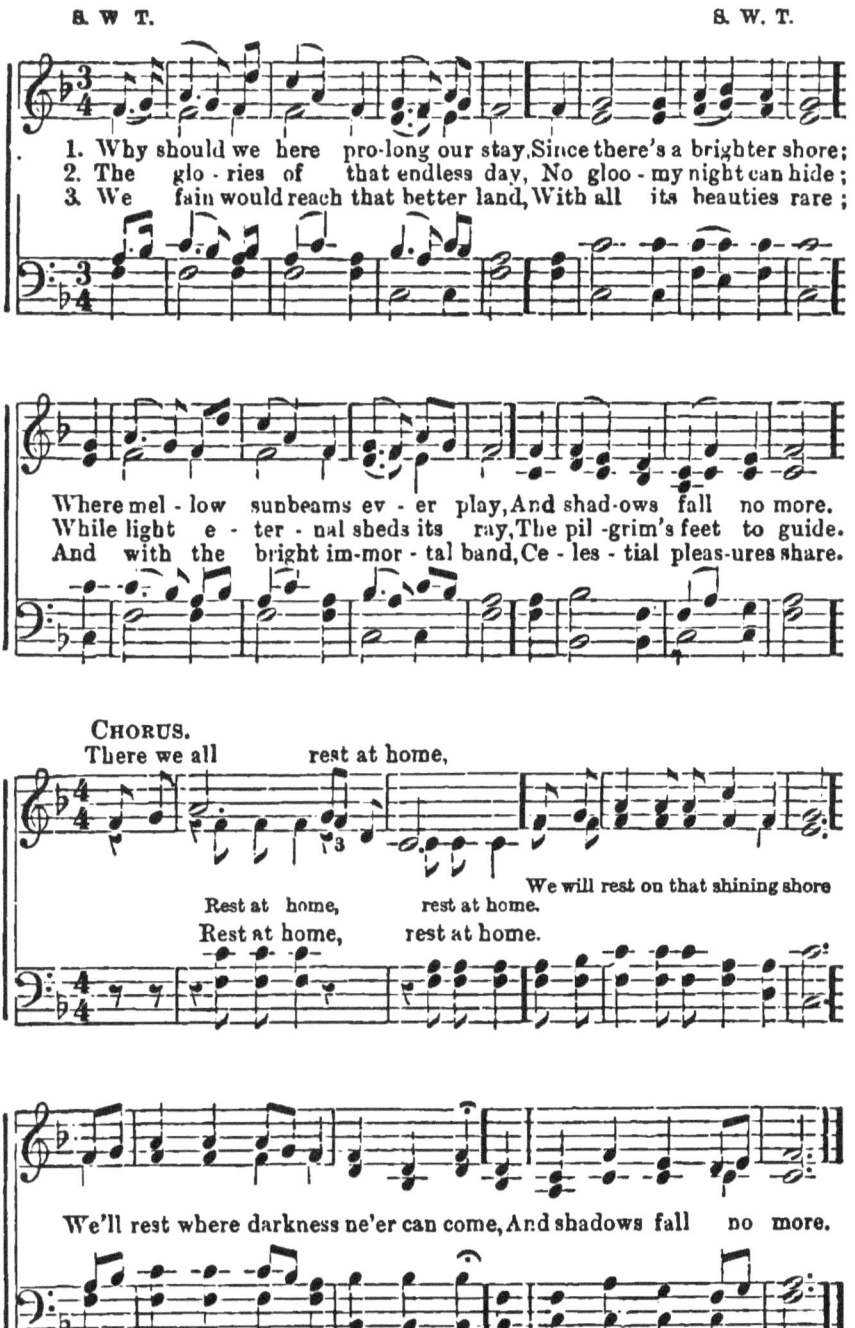

1. Why should we here pro-long our stay, Since there's a brighter shore;
2. The glo-ries of that endless day, No gloo-my night can hide;
3. We fain would reach that better land, With all its beauties rare;

Where mel-low sunbeams ev-er play, And shad-ows fall no more.
While light e-ter-nal sheds its ray, The pil-grim's feet to guide.
And with the bright im-mor-tal band, Ce-les-tial pleas-ures share.

CHORUS.
There we all rest at home,
Rest at home, rest at home.
Rest at home, rest at home.
We will rest on that shining shore

We'll rest where darkness ne'er can come, And shadows fall no more.

Almost Home.

59

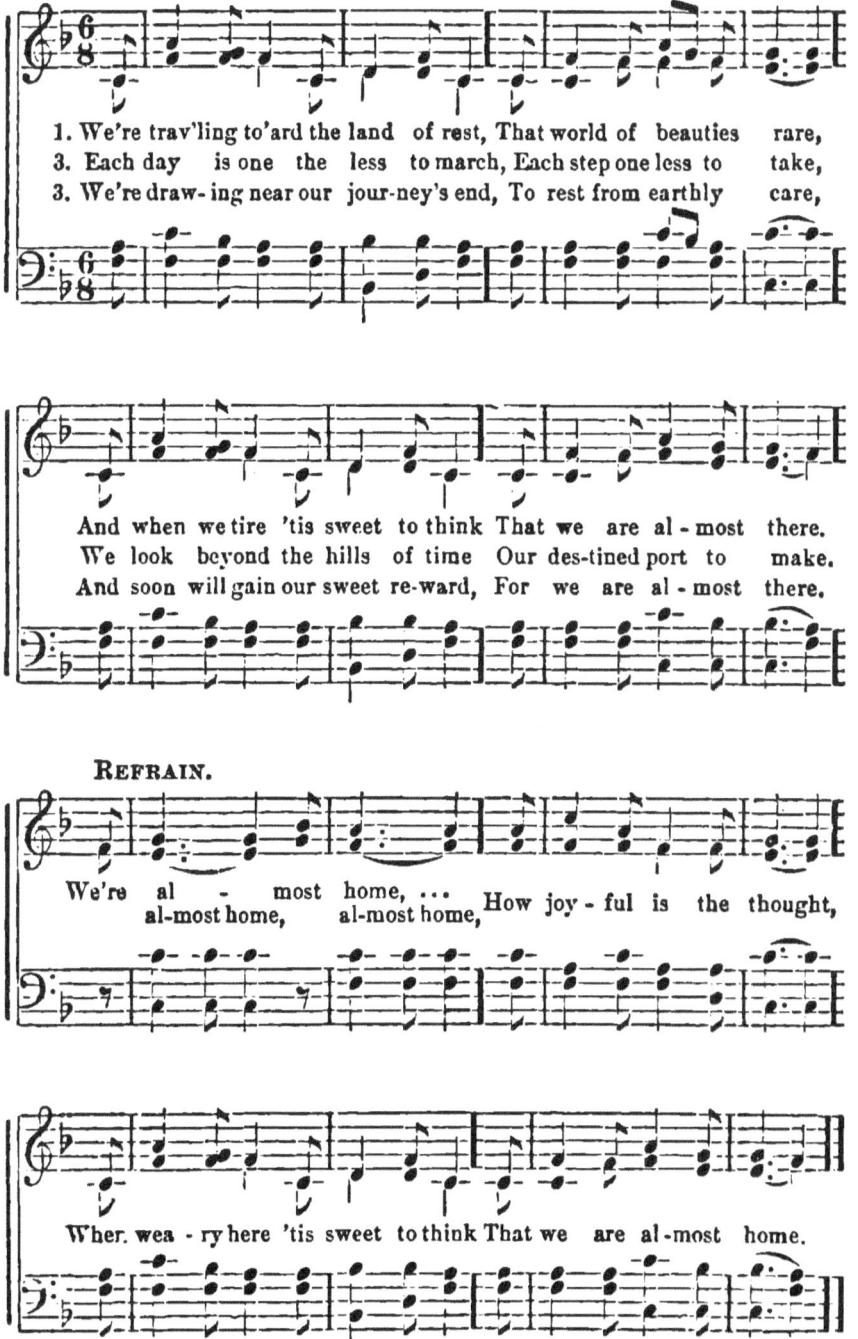

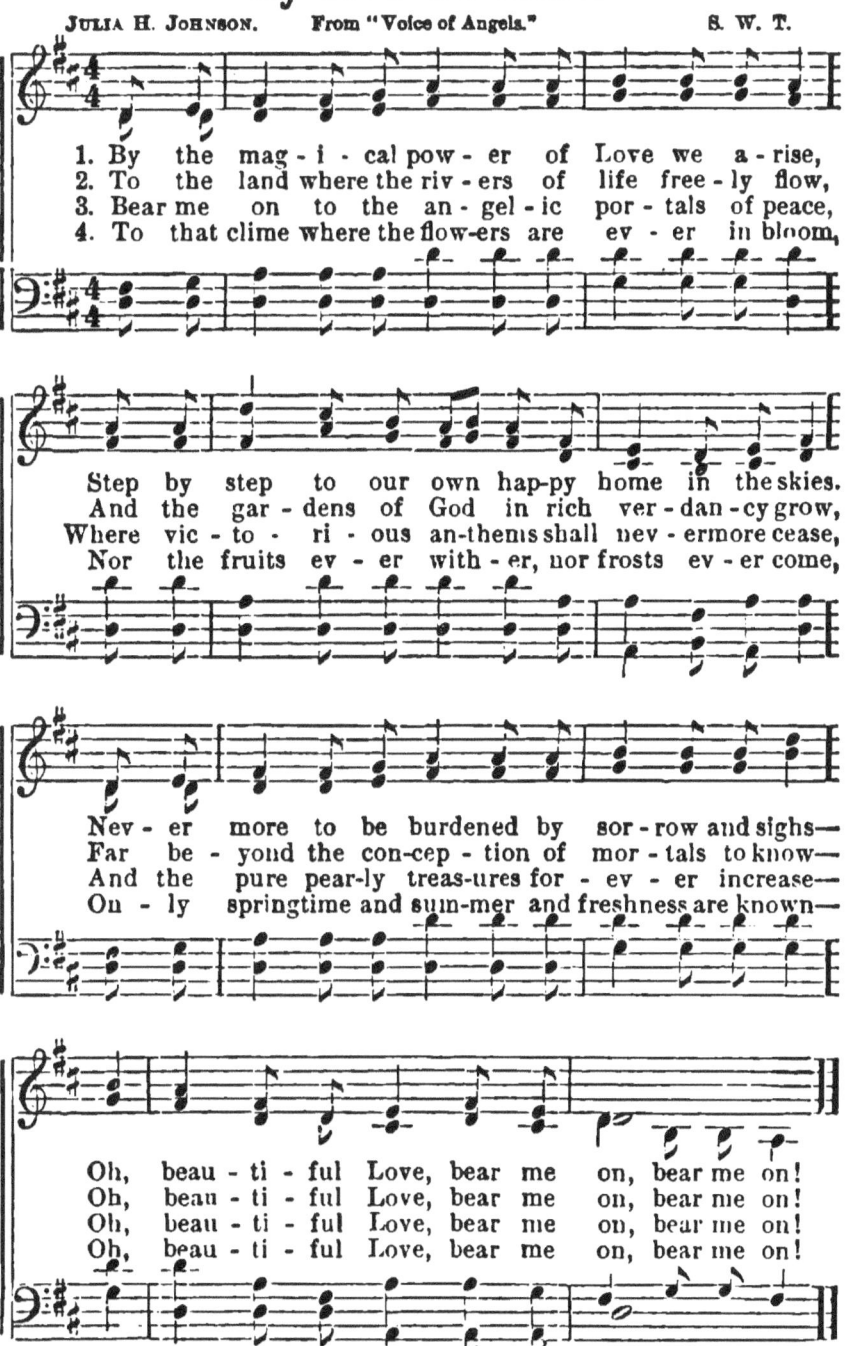

The Eden of bliss.

1. I often think, can the story be true,
When they tell of a land o'er the river;....
That's free from troubles and worldly alloy,
And where toiling is ended forever.

2. We're moving on to that happy abode,
And perhaps we may reach it to-morrow;..
When we will enter the city of rest,
Bidding farewell to earth and its sorrow.

3. O precious tho't, that when life here shall end
We will meet in those evergreen bowers;...
And pluck from gardens forever in bloom,
The refreshing and life-giving flowers.

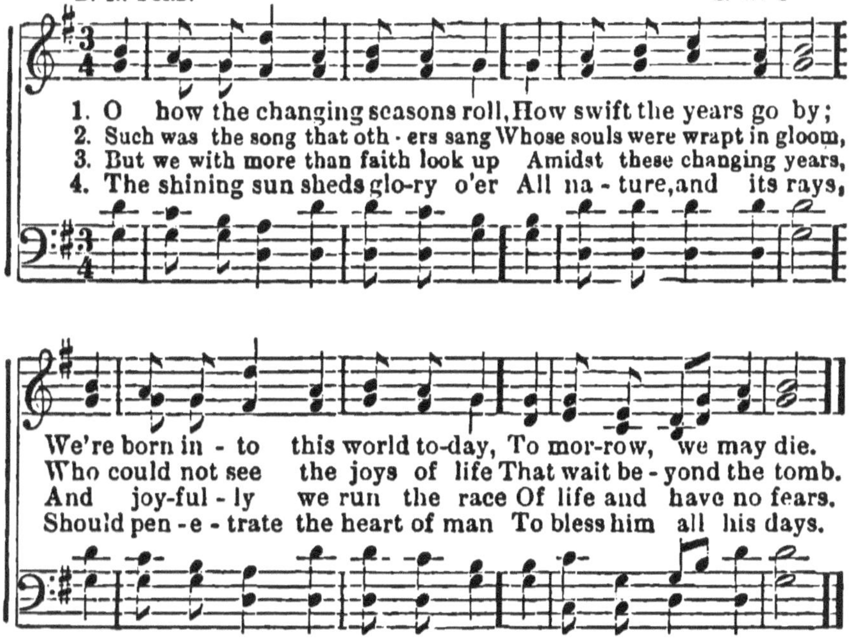

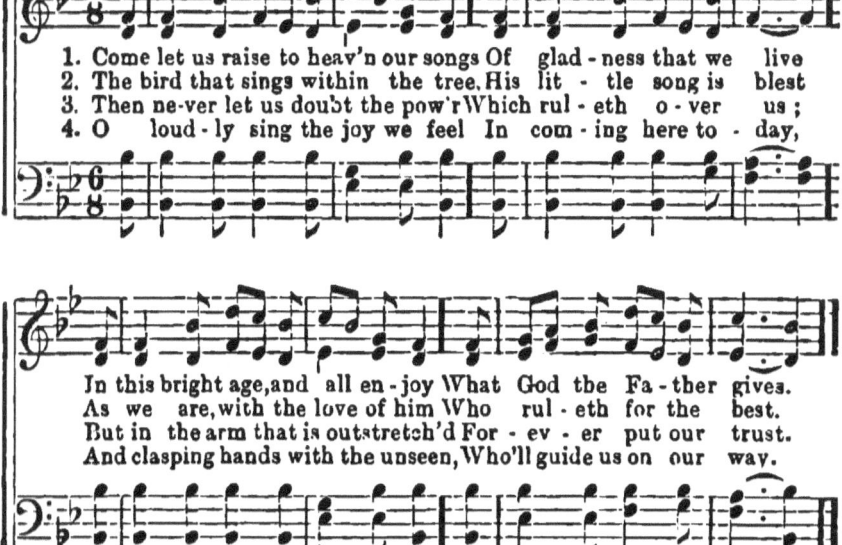

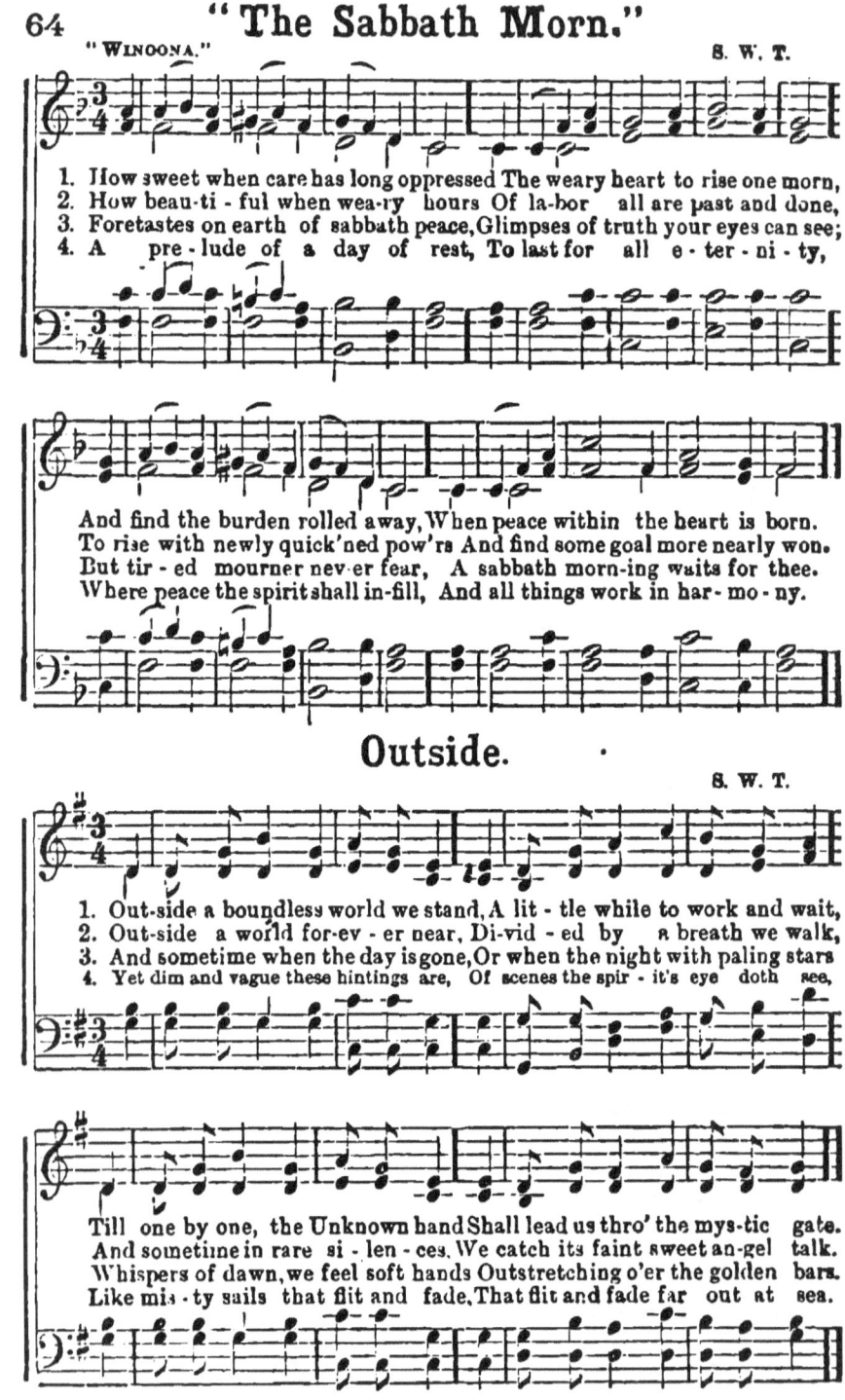

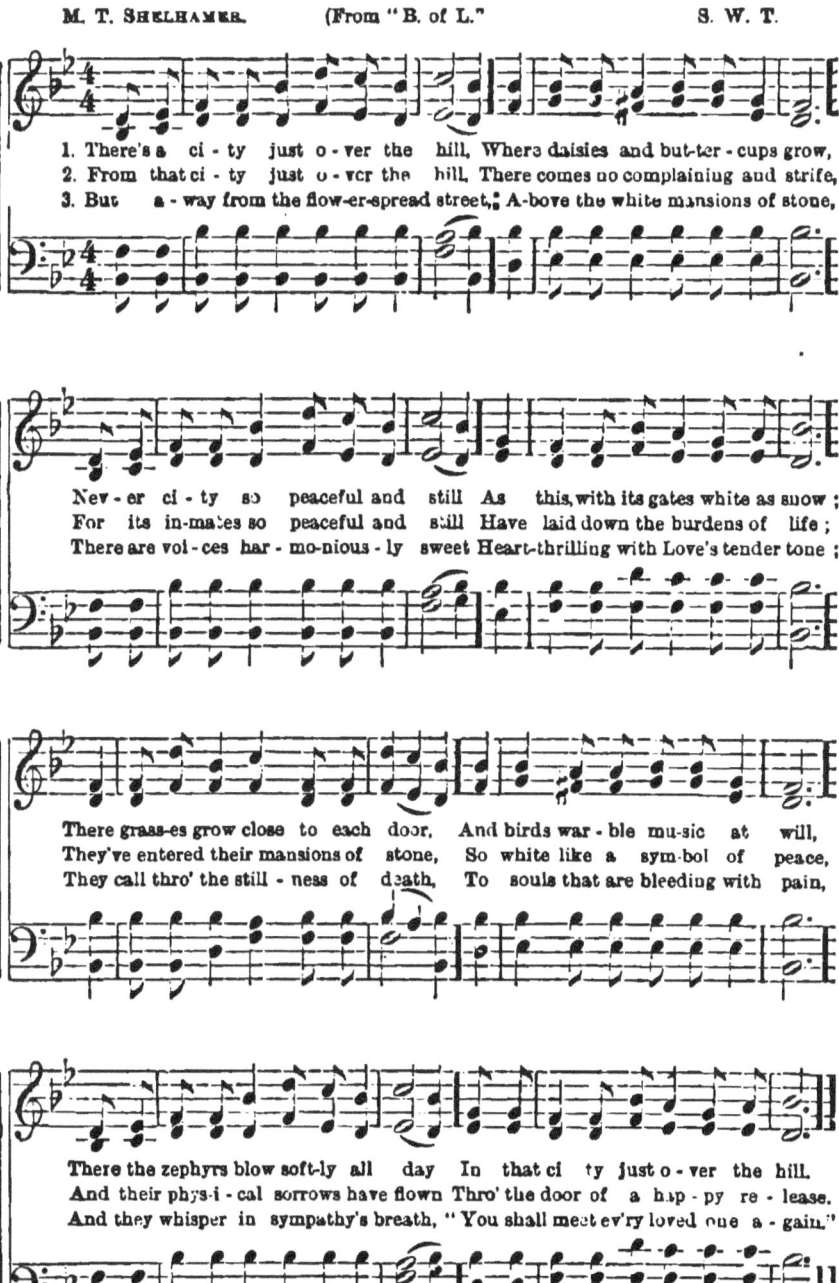

Evergreen Side.

69

S. W. T.
S. W. T.

1. How sweet is the thought that the an-gels can come,
2. No sen-ti-nels watch at those por-tals so fair,
3. A ban-quet is wait-ing and we will par-take,

To bear us a-way to their beauti-ful home;
To bar the lone pil-grim from en-ter-ing there;
When freed from this mor-tal in glo-ry to wake;

The gates of the ci-ty they'll soon o-pen wide,
But free-ly on bree-zes that heav-en-ward glide,
Then on-ward and up-ward for-ev-er we'll ride,

And bid us pass thro' to the ev-er-green side.
We'll waft o'er the stream to the ev-er-green side.
In char-i-ots bright on the ev-er-green side.

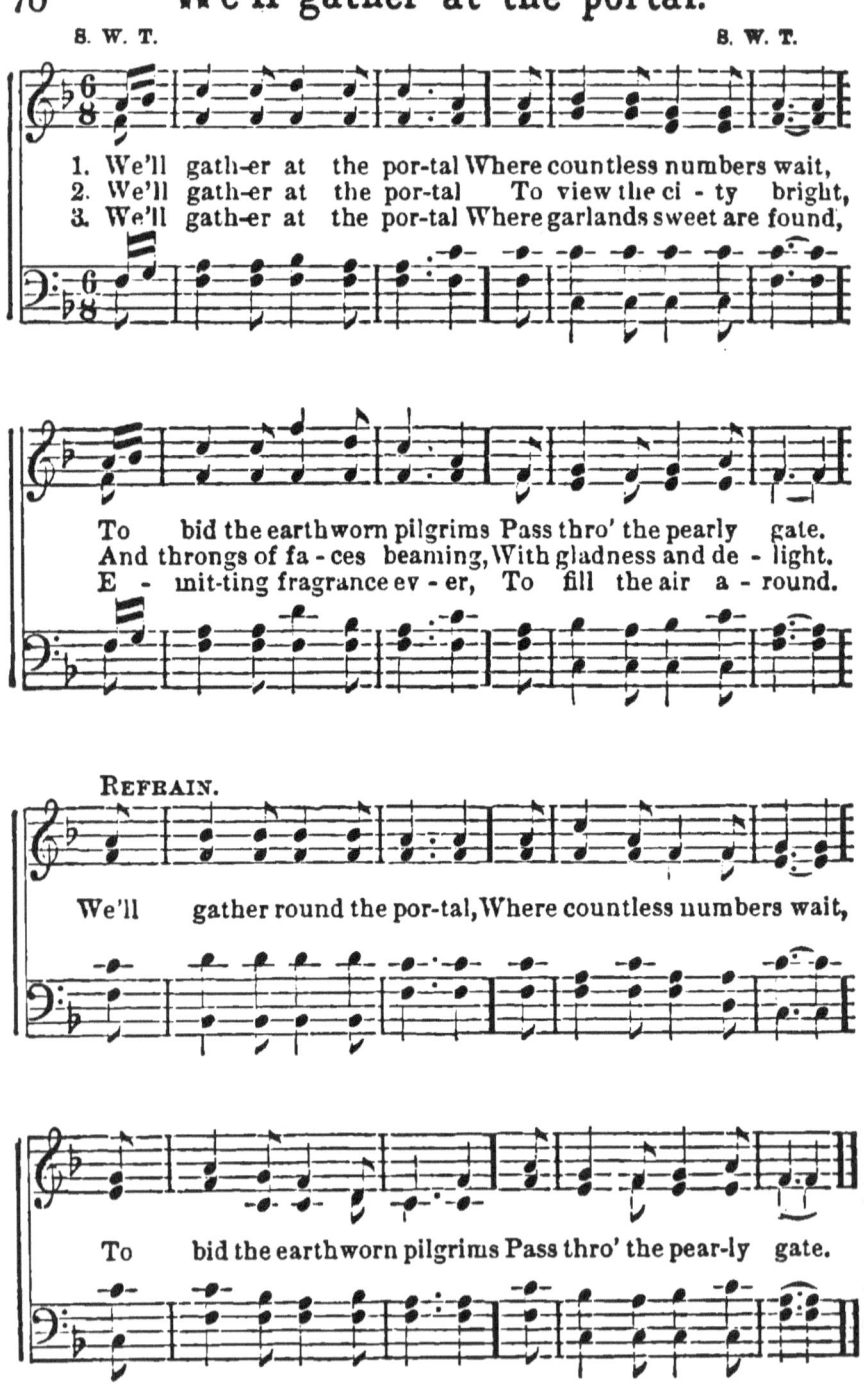

What must it be to be there.

1. We speak of the realms of the blest, That country so bright and so fair,
2. We speak of its pathways of gold, Its walls decked with jewels so rare,
3. We speak of its freedom from sin, From sor-row temptation and care,

And oft are its glo-ries confessed, But what must it be to be there?
Of wonders and pleasures untold. But what must it be to be there?
From tri-als without and with-in, But what must it be to be there?

CHORUS.

O what must it be to be there? O what must it be to be there?

We soon will arrive at the shore, And know what it is to be there.

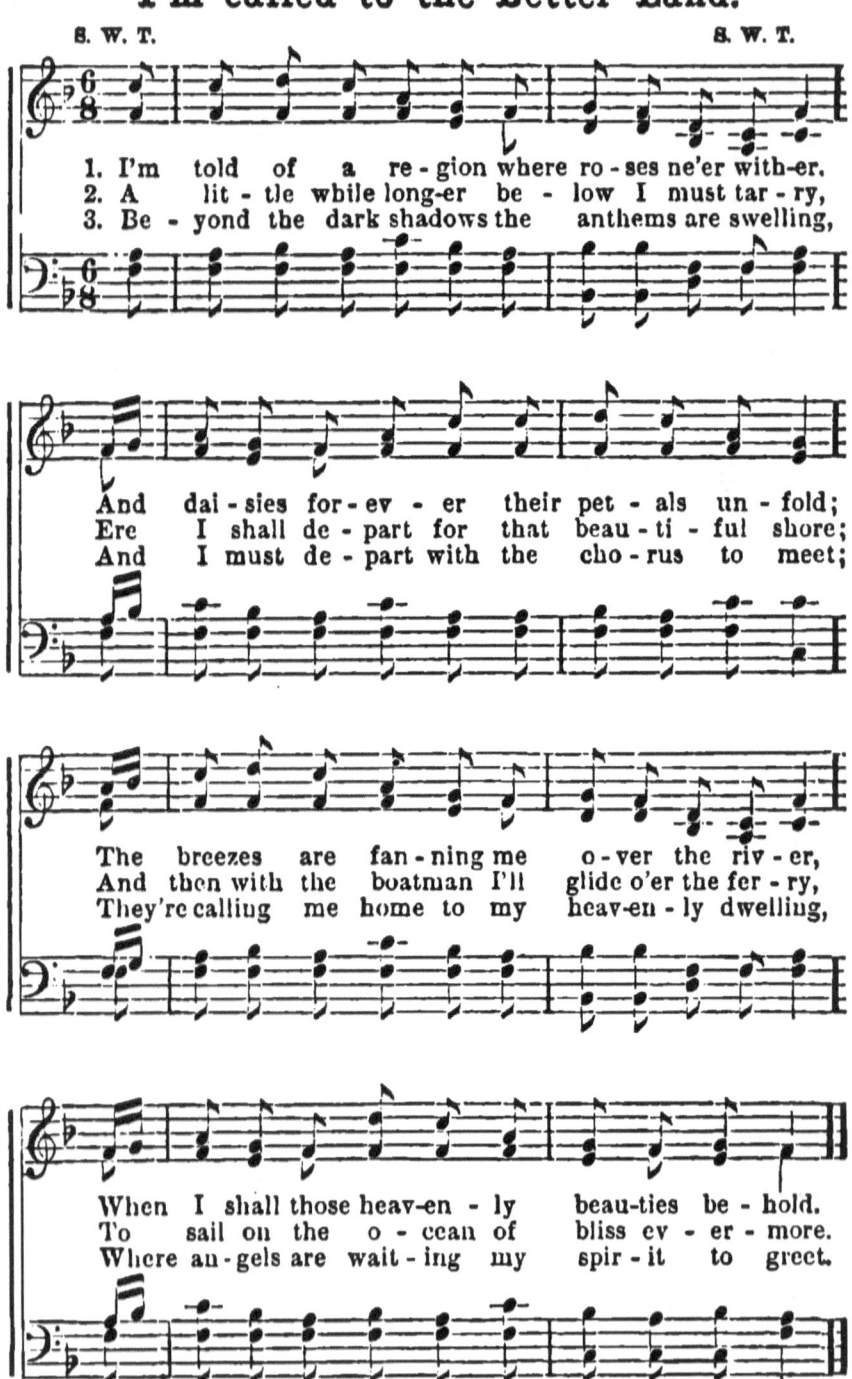

Better Land. Concluded.

The region of light.

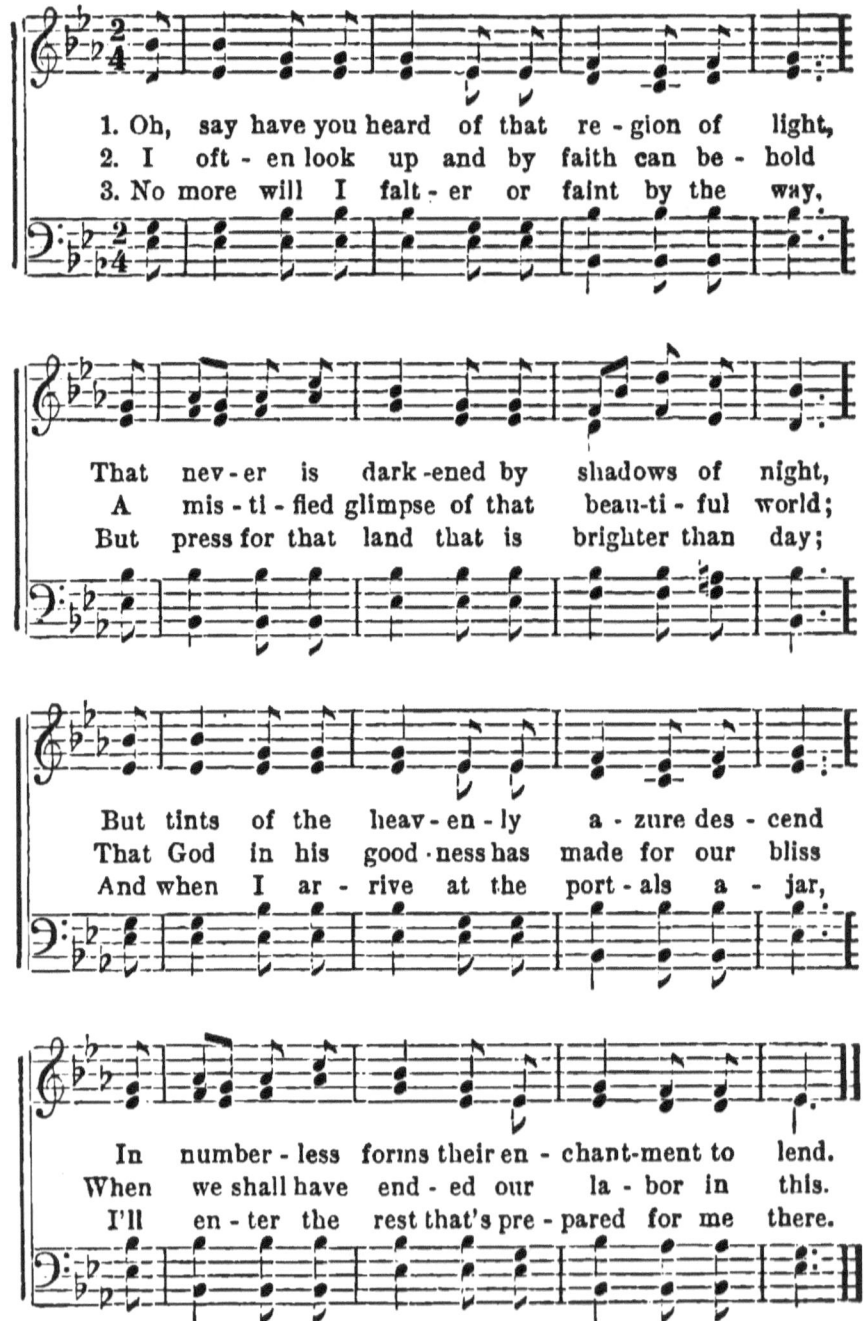

1. Oh, say have you heard of that re-gion of light,
That nev-er is dark-ened by shadows of night,
But tints of the heav-en-ly a-zure des-cend
In number-less forms their en-chant-ment to lend.

2. I oft-en look up and by faith can be-hold
A mis-ti-fied glimpse of that beau-ti-ful world;
That God in his good-ness has made for our bliss
When we shall have end-ed our la-bor in this.

3. No more will I falt-er or faint by the way,
But press for that land that is brighter than day;
And when I ar-rive at the port-als a-jar,
I'll en-ter the rest that's pre-pared for me there.

The Harvest.

1. Ho, reap-ers of life's harvest, Why stand with rusted blade,
2. Thrust in your sharpened sickle, And gath-er in the grain:
3. Come down from hill and mountain, In morning's rud-dy glow,

Until the night draws round thee, And day be-gins to fade?
The night is fast approaching, And soon will come a - gain.
Nor wait un - til the di - al Points to the noon be - low;

Why stand ye i - dle wait-ing For reap-ers more to come?
The Mas - ter calls for reap-ers; And shall he call in vain?
And come with the strong sinew, Nor faint in heat or cold;

The gold-en morn is pass-ing, Why sit ye i - dle, dumb?
Shall sheaves lie their ungathered, And waste up - on the plain?
And pause not till the even-ing Draws round its wealth of gold.

76. I long to be there.

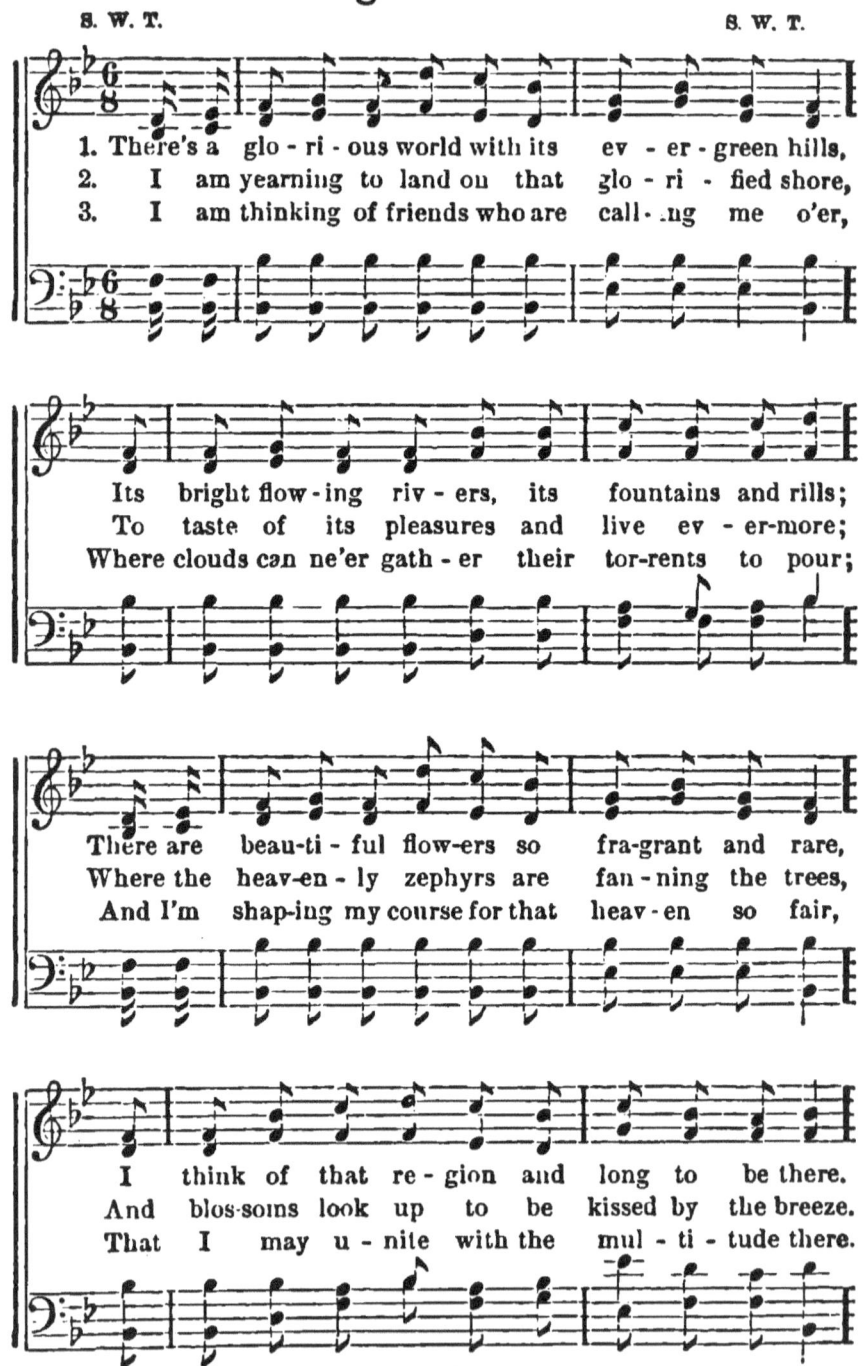

1. There's a glo-ri-ous world with its ev-er-green hills, / Its bright flow-ing riv-ers, its fountains and rills; / There are beau-ti-ful flow-ers so fra-grant and rare, / I think of that re-gion and long to be there.
2. I am yearning to land on that glo-ri-fied shore, / To taste of its pleasures and live ev-er-more; / Where the heav-en-ly zephyrs are fan-ning the trees, / And blos-soms look up to be kissed by the breeze.
3. I am thinking of friends who are call-ing me o'er, / Where clouds can ne'er gath-er their tor-rents to pour; / And I'm shap-ing my course for that heav-en so fair, / That I may u-nite with the mul-ti-tude there.

I long to be there. Concluded.

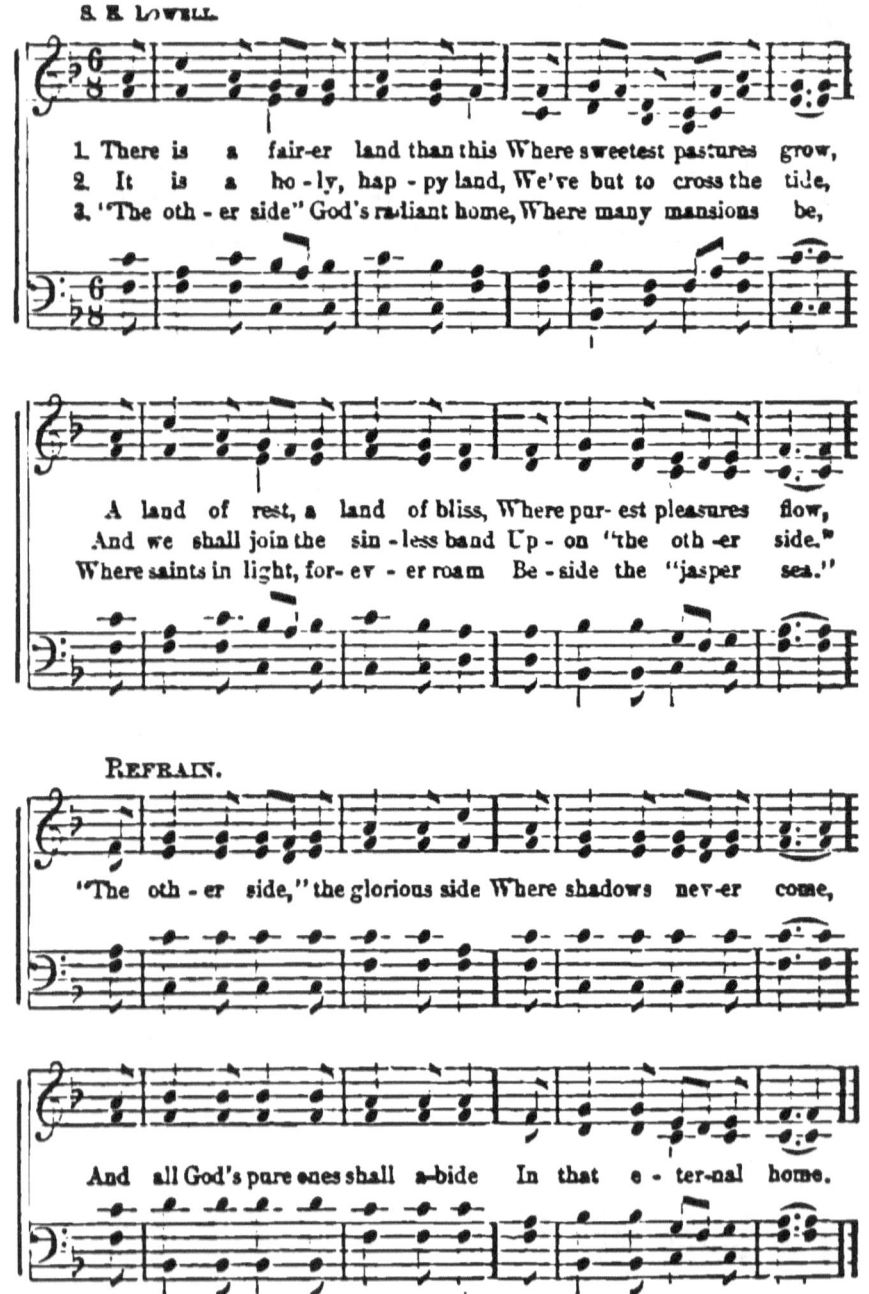

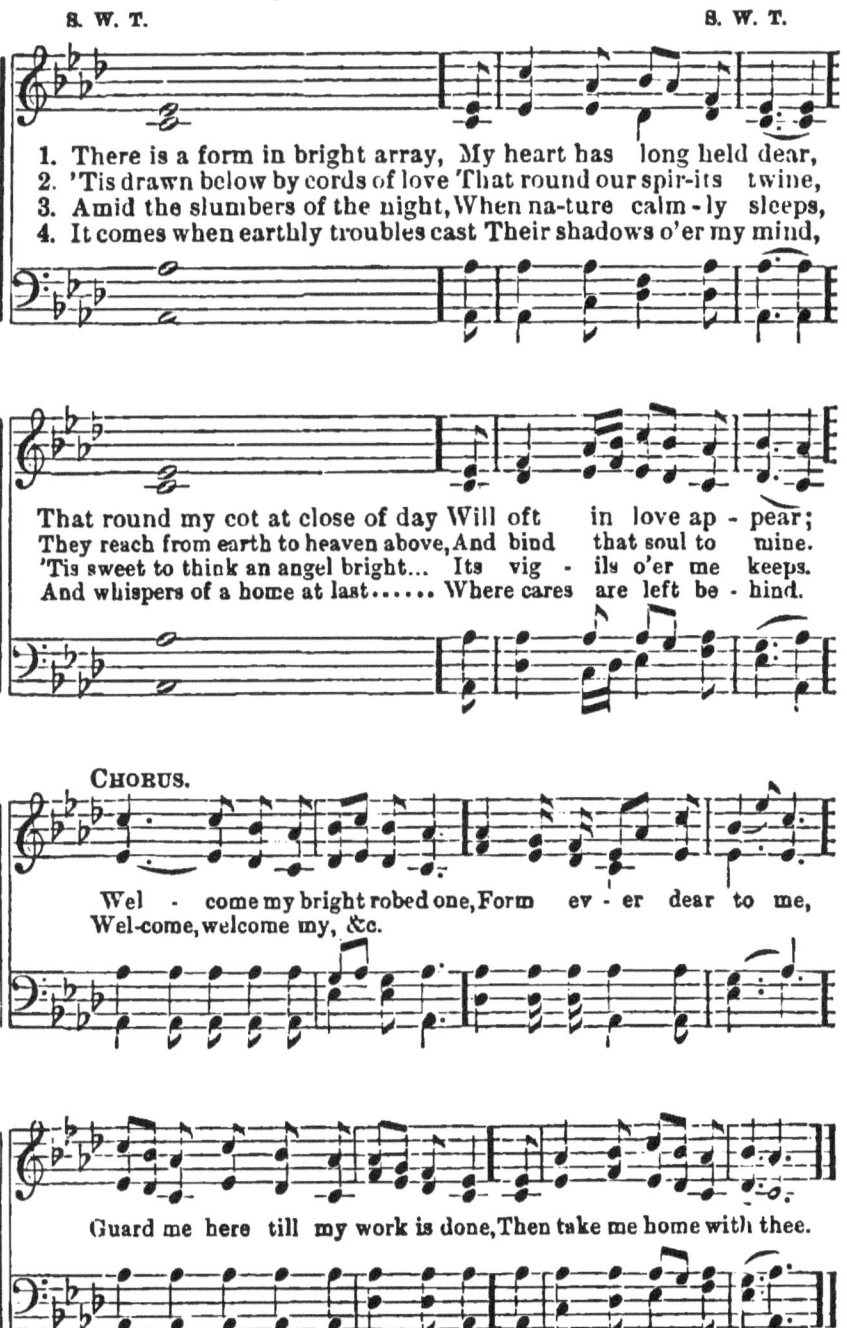

Beyond the Mortal.

Mrs. E. M. Hickok. S. W. T.

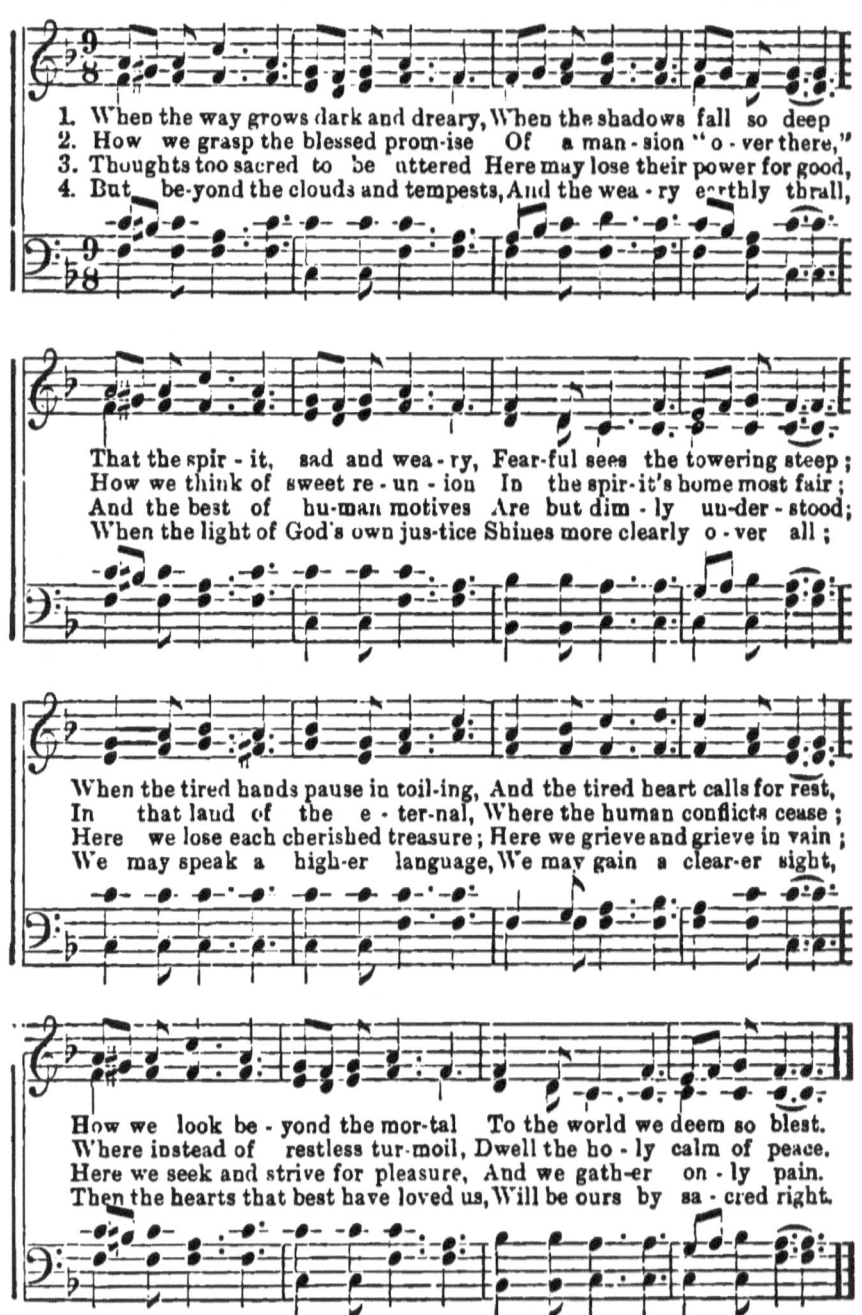

1. When the way grows dark and dreary, When the shadows fall so deep
2. How we grasp the blessed prom-ise Of a man-sion "o-ver there,"
3. Thoughts too sacred to be uttered Here may lose their power for good,
4. But be-yond the clouds and tempests, And the wea-ry earthly thrall,

That the spir-it, sad and wea-ry, Fear-ful sees the towering steep;
How we think of sweet re-un-ion In the spir-it's home most fair;
And the best of hu-man motives Are but dim-ly un-der-stood;
When the light of God's own jus-tice Shines more clearly o-ver all;

When the tired hands pause in toil-ing, And the tired heart calls for rest,
In that land of the e-ter-nal, Where the human conflicts cease;
Here we lose each cherished treasure; Here we grieve and grieve in vain;
We may speak a high-er language, We may gain a clear-er sight,

How we look be-yond the mor-tal To the world we deem so blest.
Where instead of restless tur-moil, Dwell the ho-ly calm of peace.
Here we seek and strive for pleasure, And we gath-er on-ly pain.
Then the hearts that best have loved us, Will be ours by sa-cred right.

The shining shore.

1. My days are glid-ing swift-ly, by And I a pil-gri m stran-ger,
2. We'll gird our loins, my brethren dear, Our dis-tant home dis-cern - ing;
3. Should coming days be cold and dark, We need not cease our sing- ing;

Would not de-tain them as they fly, Those hours of toil and dan -ger.
Our ab-sent Lord has left us word, Let eve-ry lamp be burn-ing.
That per-fect rest naught can molest, Where golden harps are ring-ing.

CHORUS.

For, O we stand on Jordan's strand, Our friends are passing ov - er;

And just be-fore the shining shore, We may al-most dis - cov - er.

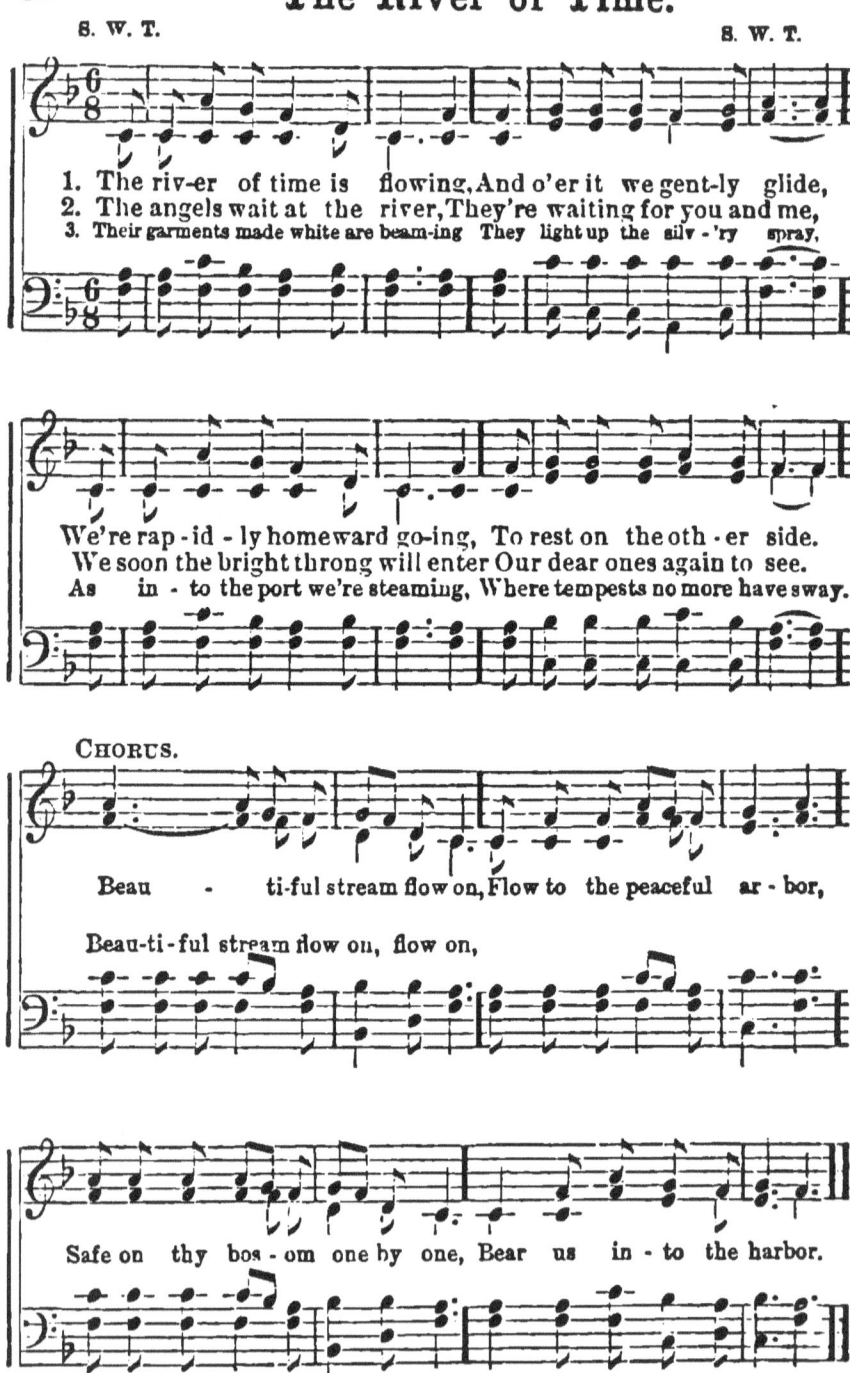

Gathered Home beyond the Sea.

A fragment.

The Angels are coming.

S. W. T. S. W. TUCKER.

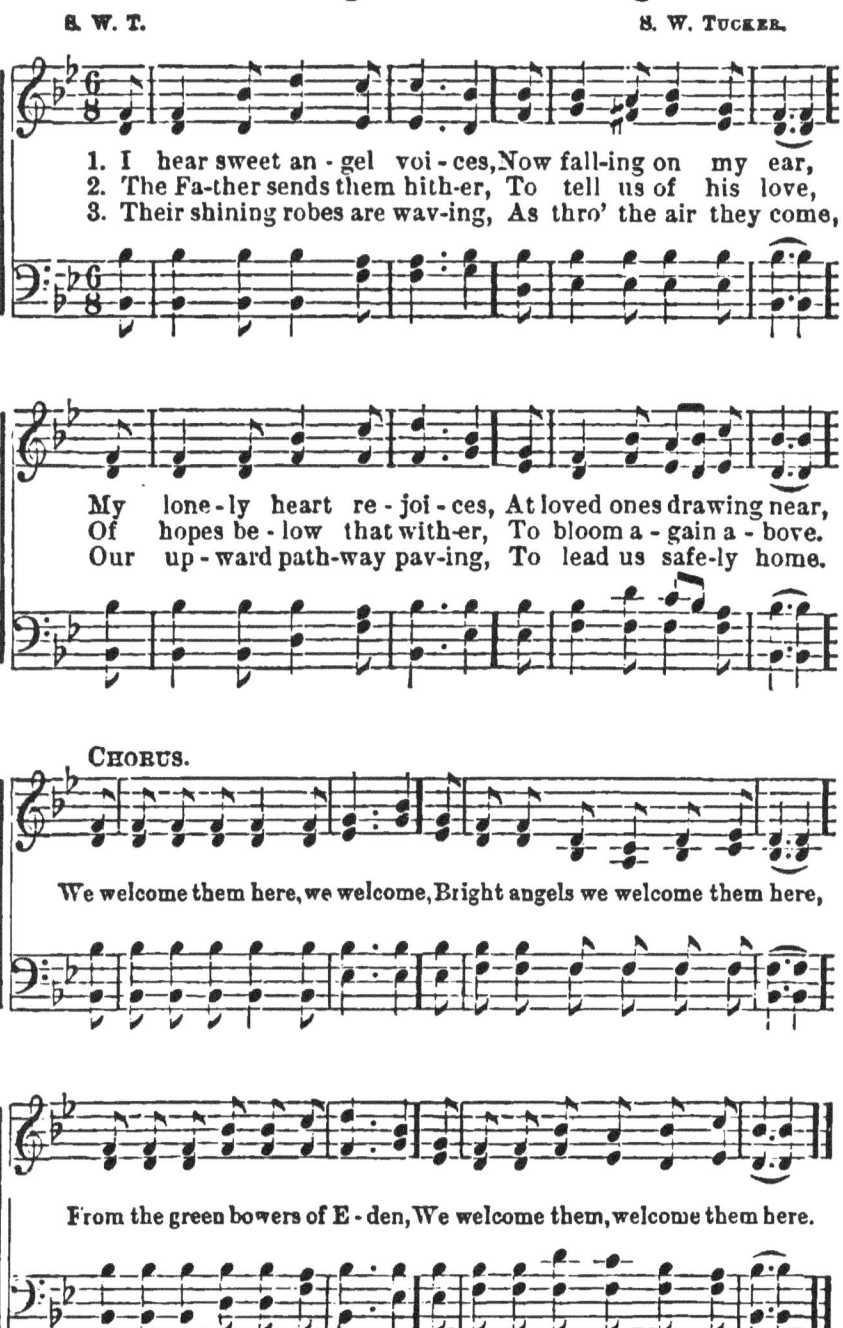

1. I hear sweet an-gel voi-ces, Now fall-ing on my ear,
   My lone-ly heart re-joi-ces, At loved ones drawing near,
2. The Fa-ther sends them hith-er, To tell us of his love,
   Of hopes be-low that with-er, To bloom a-gain a-bove.
3. Their shining robes are wav-ing, As thro' the air they come,
   Our up-ward path-way pav-ing, To lead us safe-ly home.

CHORUS.

We welcome them here, we welcome, Bright angels we welcome them here,
From the green bowers of E-den, We welcome them, welcome them here.

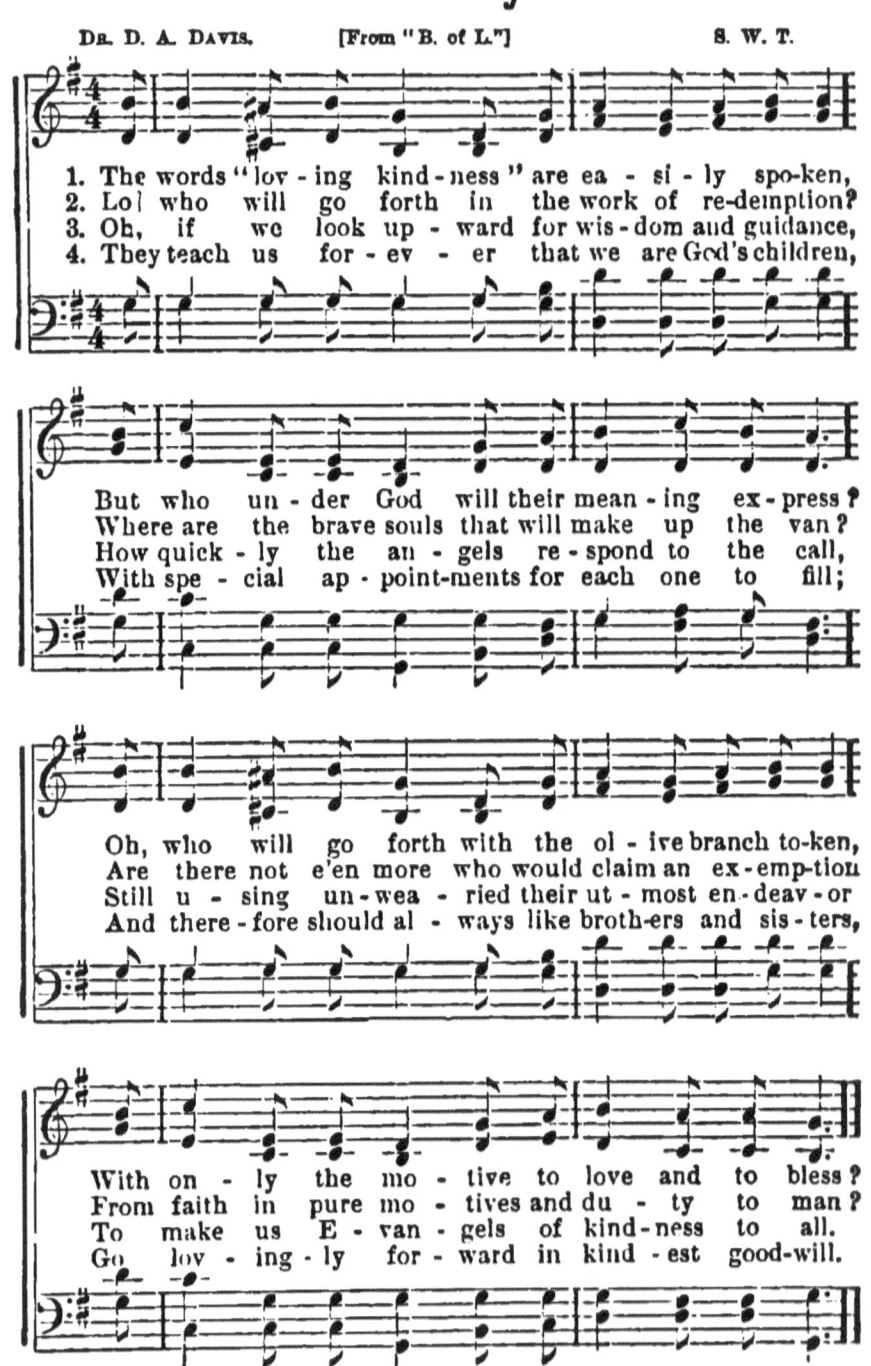

No Death.

D. N. Ford. S. W. T.

1. There is no death, all teems with life, Where-ever we may turn the eyes;
2. The bod-y back to mother earth Resolves to grow a-gain in flowers;
3. Then cheer my soul, there is no death, We live to love, and love to live;
4. No death to an - y living soul! O how my heart warms at the tho't,

Not dead is e'en the still cold form That in the cask - et shrouded lies.
And that which gave the bod-y birth Will live a-new in heavenly bowers.
And while we draw this fleeting breath, To other souls, the truth we'll give.
E - ter-nal life to us un - folds, With joys ce-lest - ial ever fraught.

Star of Truth.

D. N. Ford.

1. See how the gold-en star doth rise, How beauti - ful its ray;
2. The stars that in the heavens are fixed, Shine forth with twinkling rays,
3. It is a sun we gaze up - on, The light is all its own,
4. That brilliant sun, whose streaming fire Is seen so far a - way,

It her-alds to a darkened world, The com-ing of the day.
But this bright star with steady light E - ter - nal - ly will blaze.
It was a spark, like lightning sent From off the gold-en throne.
Shall nev-er wane, but al-ways light Earth's pilgrim on his way.

O bear me away.

S. W. T.

1. O bear me a-way to the realms of the blest,
My spir-it is wea-ry and long-ing for rest,
I fain would u-nite with the an-gel-ic band,
And share the re-pose of that beau-ti-ful land.

2. O bear me a-way with the an-gels to dwell,
E'en now they in-vite me their num-bers to swell,
They beck-on to me from that ra-di-ant shore,
And wait for the boat-man to car-ry me o'er.

3. O bear me a-way to my fi-nal a-bode,
And give me re-lief from this wea-ri-some load,
For I can no long-er this bur-den en-dure,
I seek one that's light-er, im-mor-tal and pure.

Live for an Object.

D. N. Ford.   S. W. T.

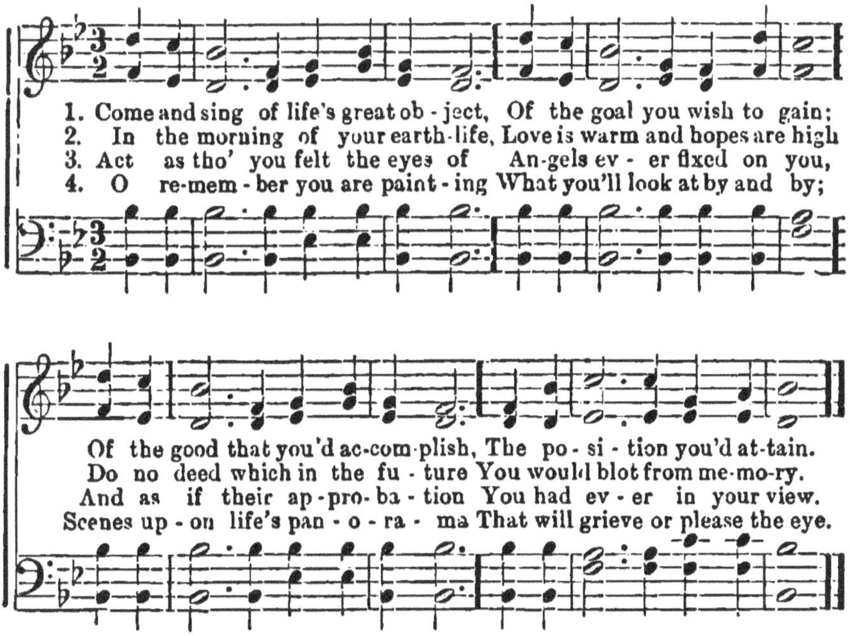

1. Come and sing of life's great ob-ject, Of the goal you wish to gain;
2. In the morning of your earth-life, Love is warm and hopes are high
3. Act as tho' you felt the eyes of An-gels ev - er fixed on you,
4. O re-mem - ber you are paint-ing What you'll look at by and by;

Of the good that you'd ac-com-plish, The po - si - tion you'd at-tain.
Do no deed which in the fu - ture You would blot from me-mo-ry.
And as if their ap-pro-ba - tion You had ev - er in your view.
Scenes up - on life's pan - o - ra - ma That will grieve or please the eye.

Golden Shore.

S. W. T.   S. W. T.

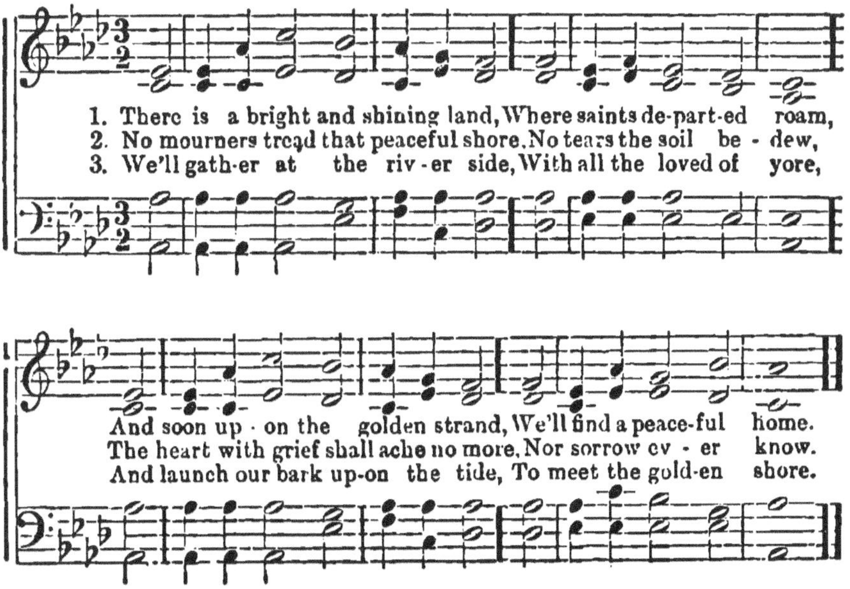

1. There is a bright and shining land, Where saints de-part-ed roam,
2. No mourners tread that peaceful shore. No tears the soil be - dew,
3. We'll gath-er at the riv-er side, With all the loved of yore,

And soon up - on the golden strand, We'll find a peace-ful home.
The heart with grief shall ache no more, Nor sorrow ev - er know.
And launch our bark up-on the tide, To meet the gold-en shore.

Silent Help.

EDNA C. SMITH.   S. W. T.

1. Sitting in my silent chamber, Or at night up-on my bed,
2. Gentle hand and shad'wy fingers, For the shape I can-not see,
3. Then I turn from heartfelt sorrow, For a-while for-get my pain,
4. Onward, upward, till life closes, And I lay my bur-den by,

Oft I feel a gen-tle pressure Of a hand up-on my head.
Touch that speaks of tender pi-ty, Which is all the world to me.
Drinking in the heav'nly counsel Which comes floating o'er my brain.
Till my soul released from prison, Seeks its home and rest on high.

He's Gone.

G. W. BARNES.   S. W. T.

1. A good man to his rest has gone, A husband true as po-lar star,
2. Peace, sweetest peace be to his soul, And fragrant } mem-'ry be ;
    may his
3. O mourning hearts! let light break thro' The sa-} grief pro-found,
    ble clouds of
4. So that this pilgrimage may show In days to come a sol-ace sweet,

A father whose affections won The love of him that naught could mar.
He's fou't the fight, and gained the goal Of unalloyed e-ter-ni-ty.
And give the weeping eyes a view Of glories that in heaven a-bound.
Of faith, that each at length shall know } loved in bliss to meet.
    The joy the

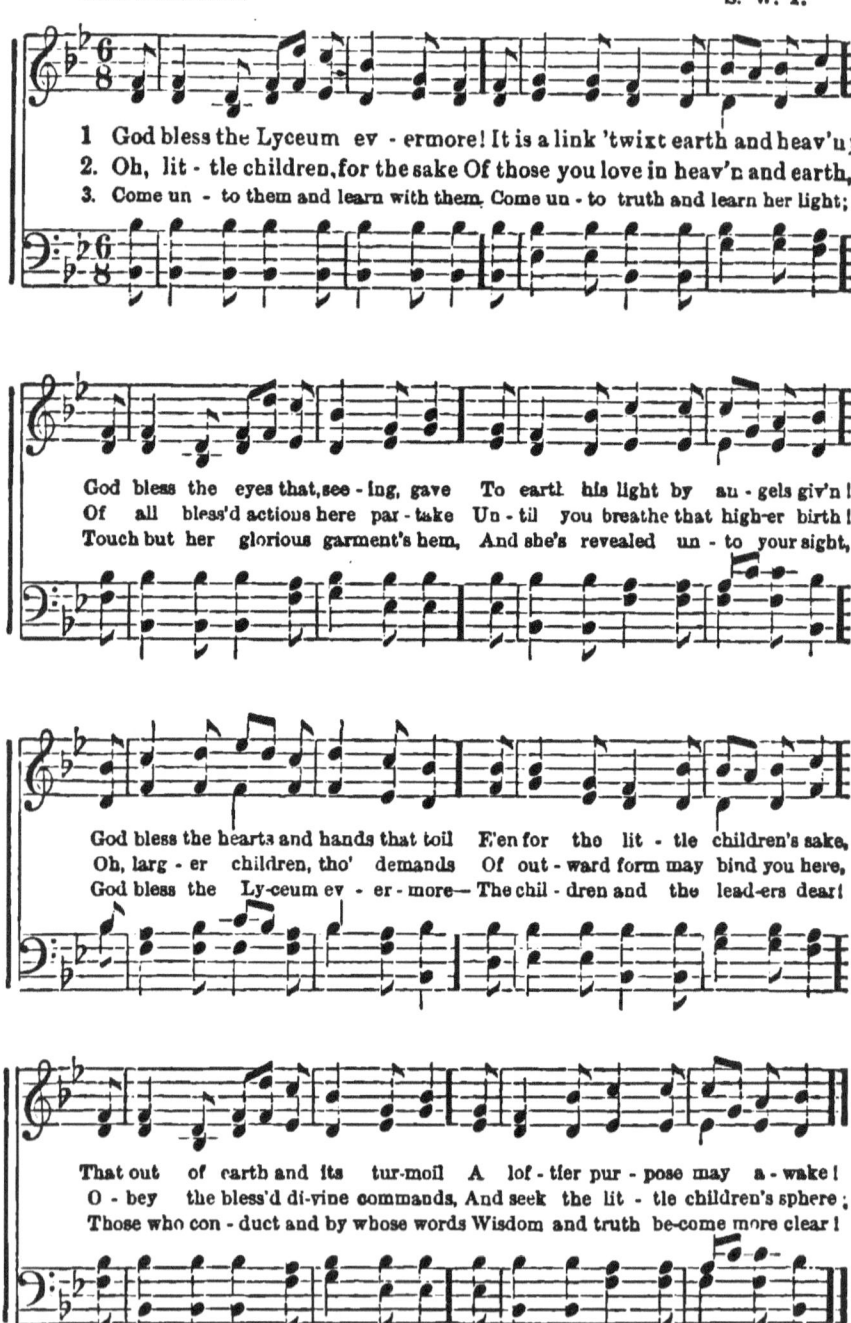

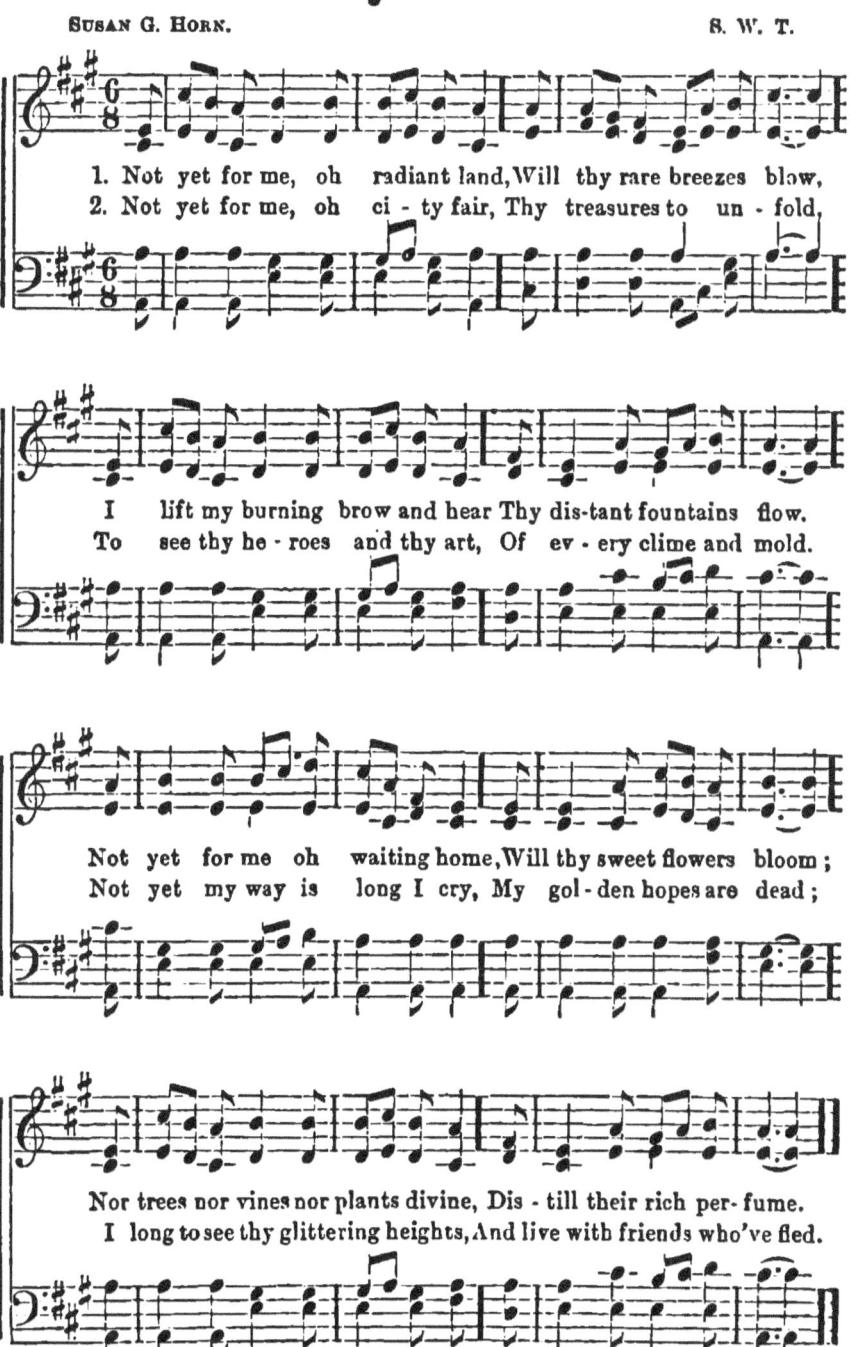

They are coming.

1. Angels are coming with words of love, Coming our hearts to cheer,
Bearing good news from the world above, Down to the pilgrims here;
Gentle as breezes of heaven they come, Messengers from on high,
Breathing a tale of their shining home, Under a cloudless sky.

2. As we look o-ver the stream we see Flitting before our sight,
Forms that are dearer than life can be, Robed in their pearly white;
Often they're with us our tears to dry, Bidding us weep no more,
Since the departed for whom we sigh, Live on the better shore.

3. Soon with the bright ones we'll take our flight, Forming a happy band,
Bound for the world of e-ternal light, Up in the spirit land;
When we arrive at the city fair, With its celestial dome,
We'll see a dwelling erected there, For our immortal home.

Passed On.

S. W. T. S. W. T.

1. Another voice is hushed and still, Another | dear one | gone,
2. The Father called the spirit home, From chains that | bound it | here,
3. Another one will meet us there, When we too | cross the | stream,
4. The debt of nature now is paid. Disease its | work has | done,

No more her wonted seat to fill, Or | join our | so - cial | song.
That with the angels it might roam, Thro' | his ce- | les - tial | sphere.
To breathe that sweet and balmy air Where | lights im- | mor-tal | gleam.
The soul no more thro' grief can wade, Or | dwell where | troubles | come.

Angel visitants.

S. W. T. S. W. T.

1. How oft to earth the loved ones come, To tell us of their heav'nly home.
2. They drive our grief and care a-way, And light-en bur-dens of the day,
3. They tell us of the joys that flow, Be-yond this storm-y vale be-low.

They whis-per words of love, and cheer, That dis - si - pate our gloom and fear.
They o'er us watch-ful vi - gils keep, And fan our wea-ry eyes to sleep.
And that they'll soon conduct us there, The bless-ings of that world to share.

Come go with me.

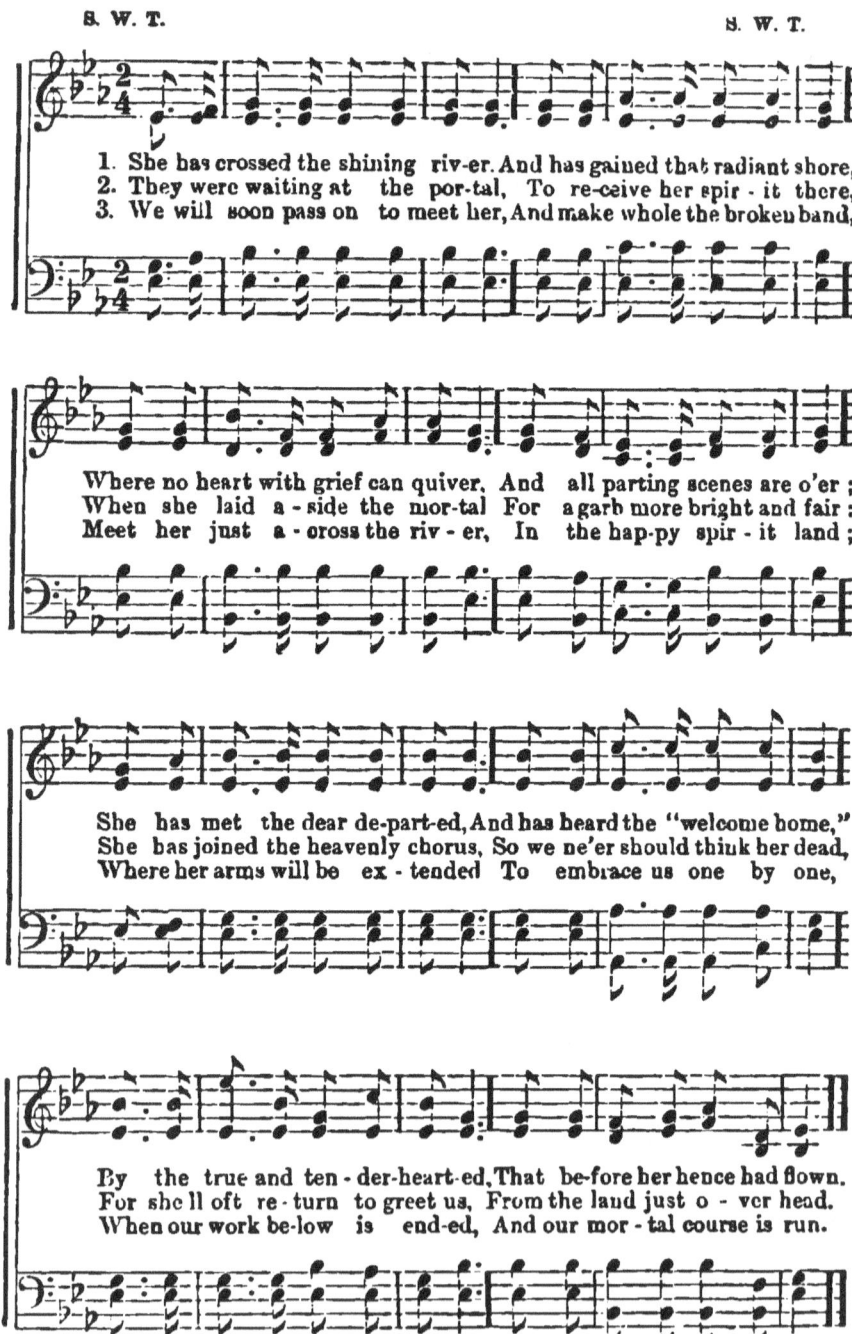

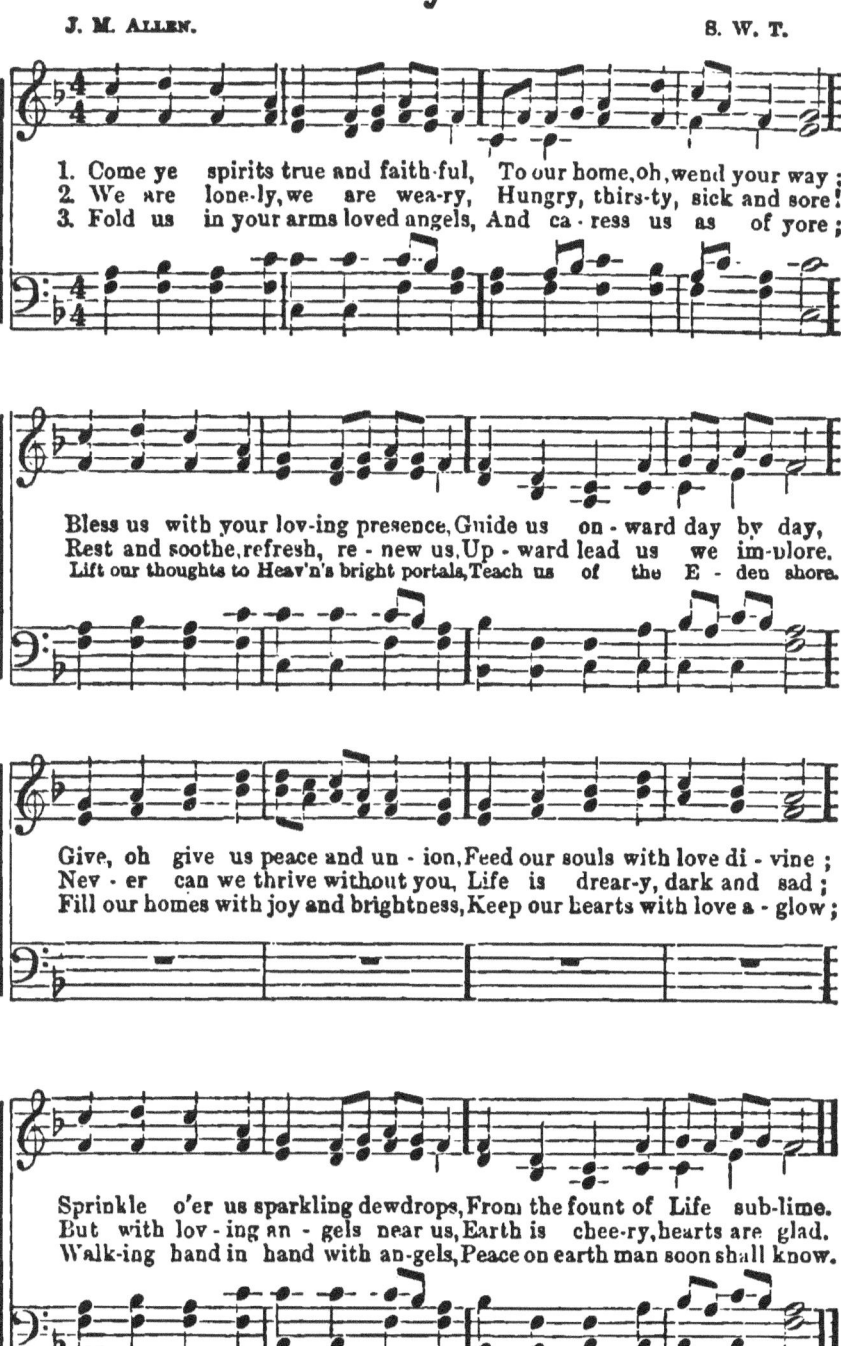

Waiting to go.

S. W. T. S. W. T.

1. We are waiting for the murmur Of these chil-ly winds to cease,
2. We are waiting for the moment, When we'll say to earth farewell,
3. We are waiting for the dimness, To creep o'er our mor-tal eyes,

We are wait-ing that the Father, May our souls from earth release:
We are wait-ing for the an-gels, To re-move us home to dwell;
We are wait-ing for a message, From the world a-bove the skies;

Then be-yond the foam-ing bill-ows, We will tread the em'-rald sand
Where the trees with fruit are la-den, Nev-er more to know de-cay,
For the welcome word come high-er, Come and rest from toil and care,

Where no clouds the light can darken, Or be-dim the shin-ing strand.
And the bow'rs with green are waving, Brighter than the tints of May.
Ye who've worked with hands most willing, For a crown a-bove to wear.

Summary days are coming.

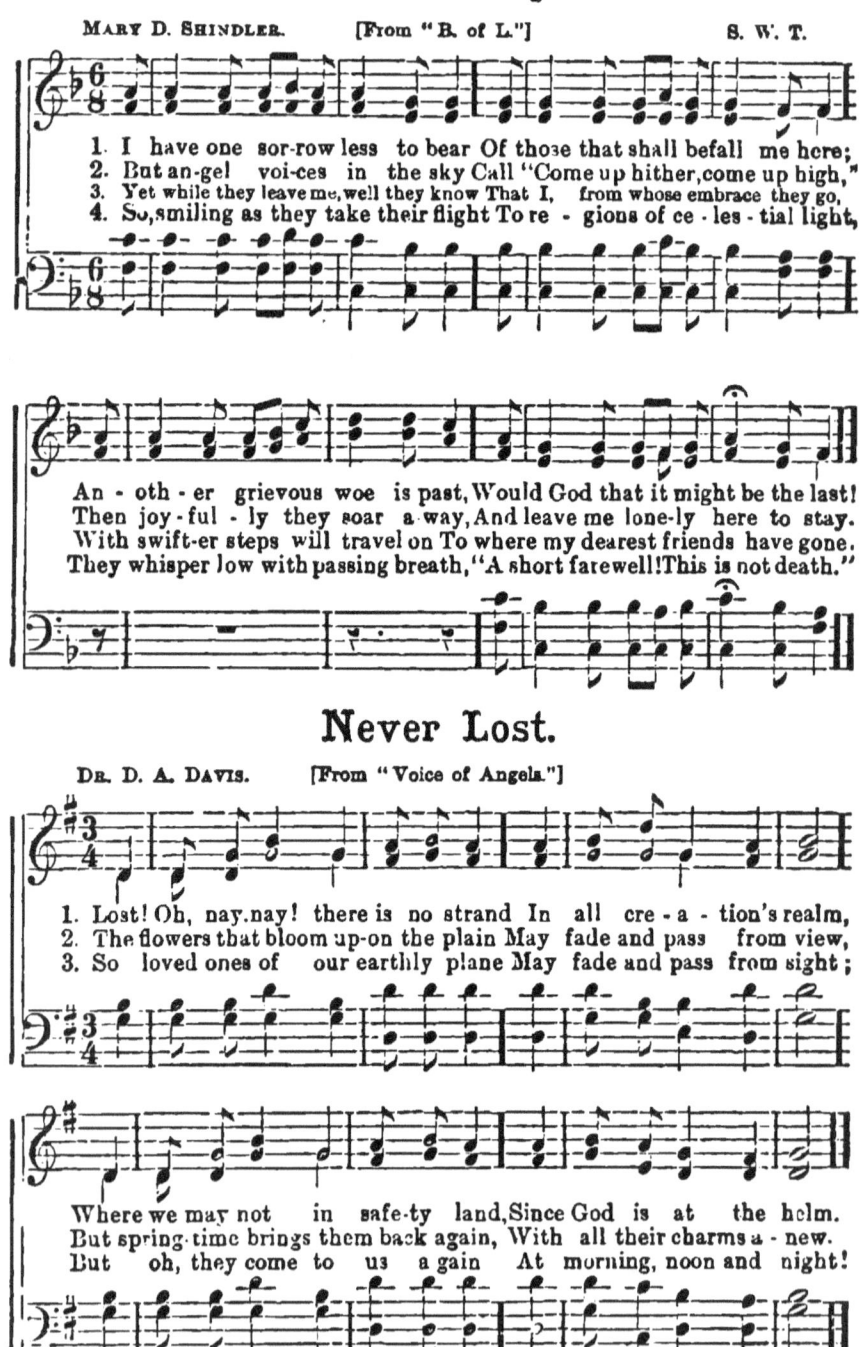

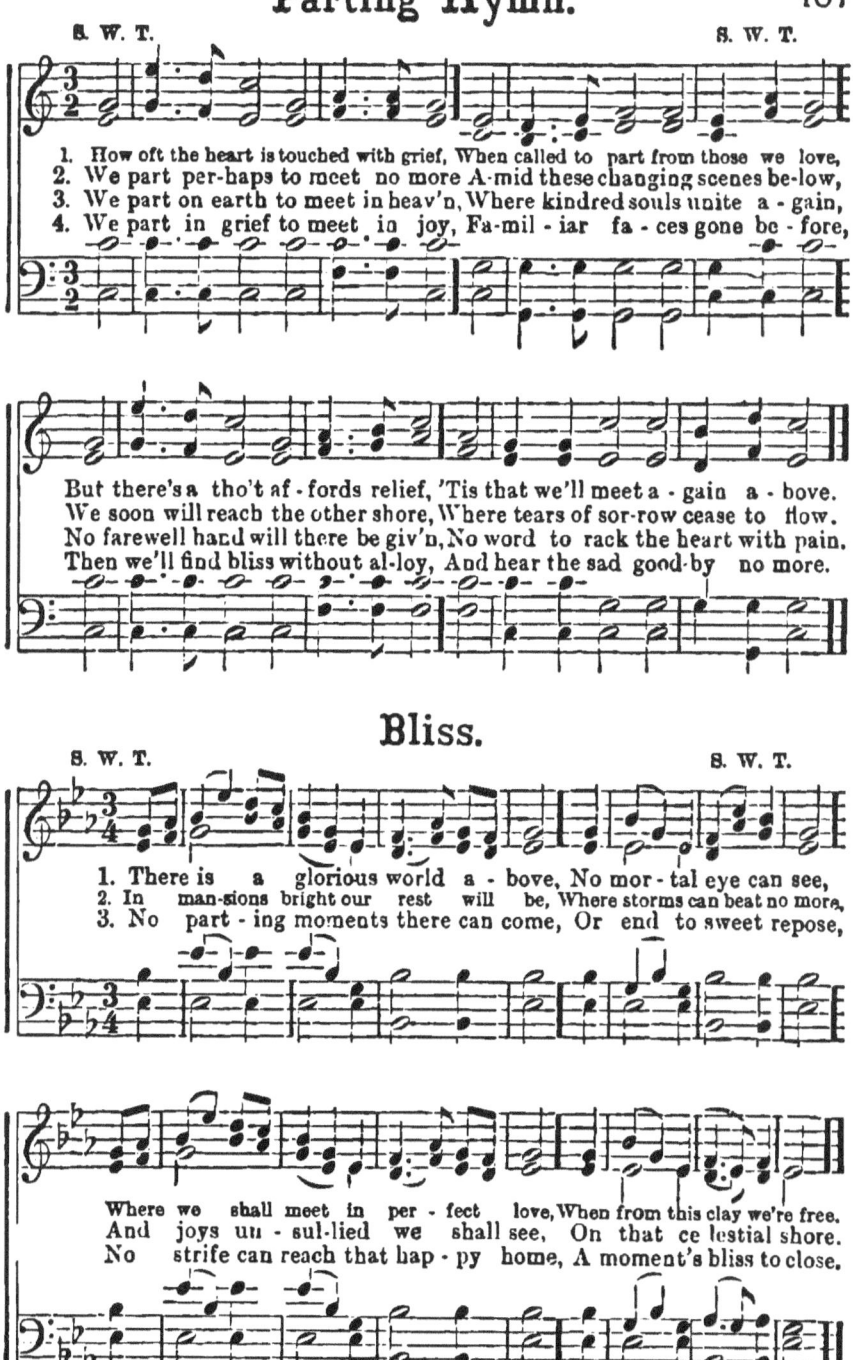

Waiting at the river.

S. W. T.

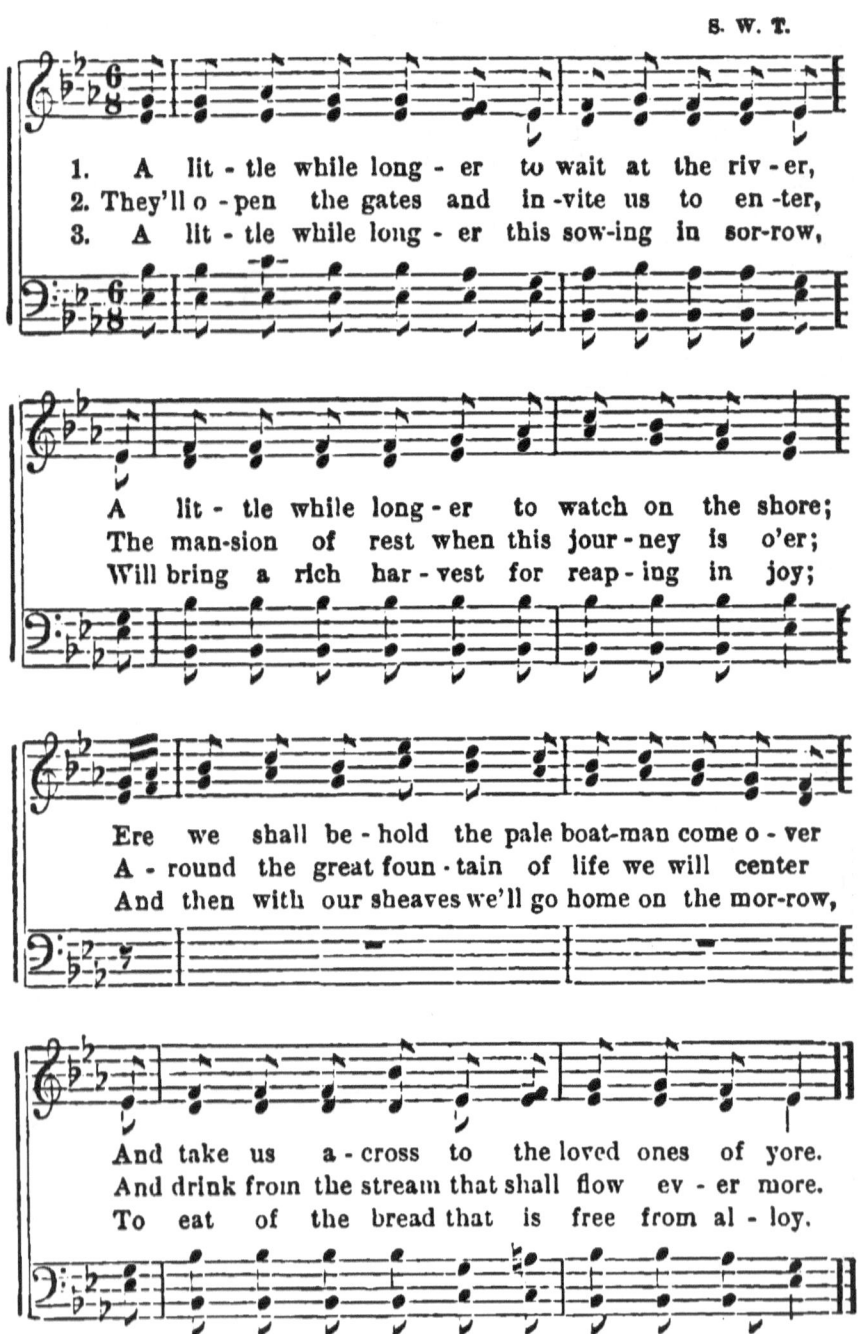

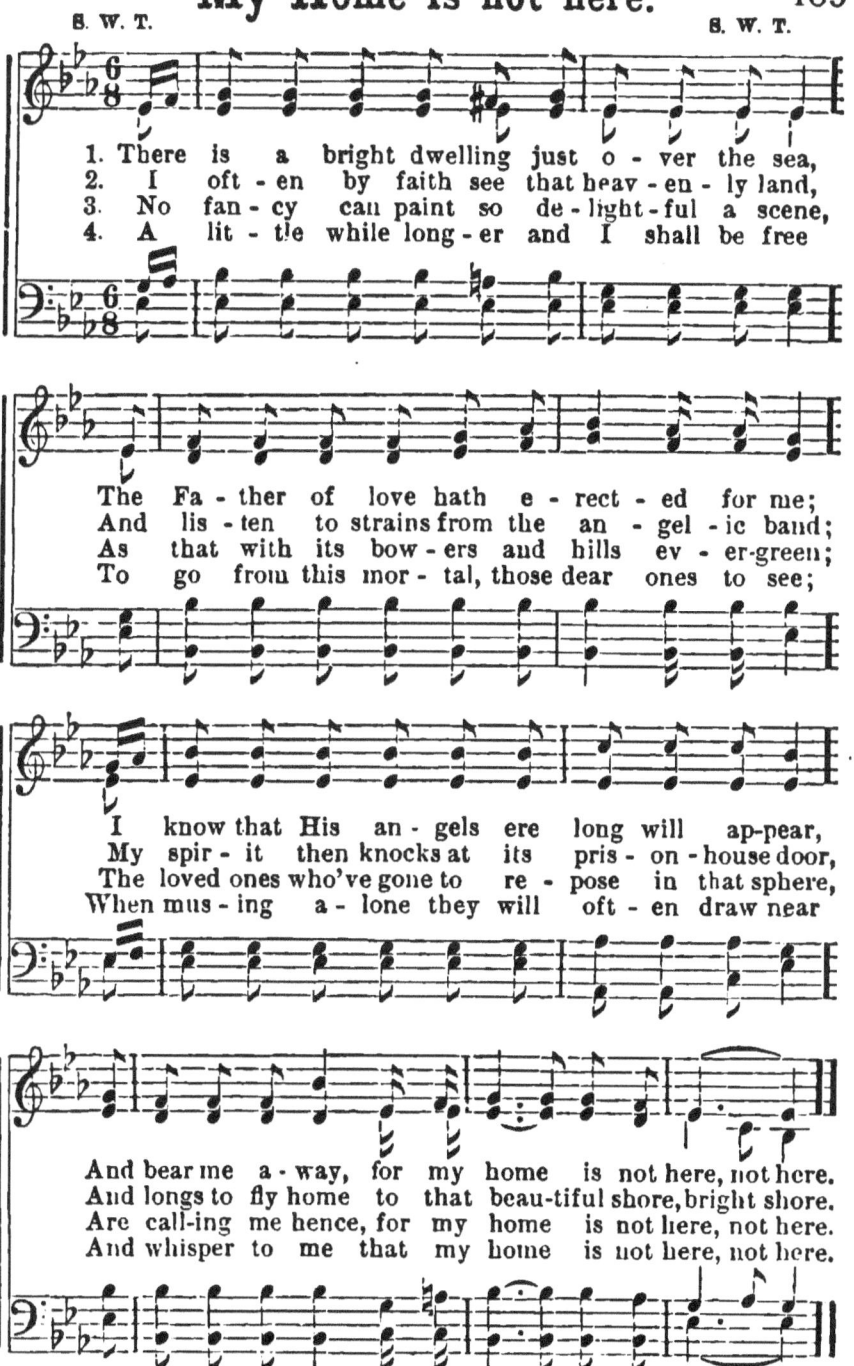

Waiting on this Shore.

The Eden Above.

1. We're bound for the land of the pure and the ho-ly,
2. In that bless-ed land nei-ther sigh-ing nor an-guish,
3. Each saint has a man-sion pre-pared and all furnished,
4. March on hap-py pil-grims, the land is be-fore you,

The home of the hap-py, the king-dom of love;
Can breathe in the fields where the glo-ri-fied move;
Ere from this clay house he is summoned to move;
And soon its ten thou-sand de-lights we shall prove;

Ye wan-d'rers from God, in the broad road of fol-ly,
Ye heart-bur-dened ones, who in mis-er-y languish,
Its gates and its tow-ers with glo-ry are burnished,
Yes, soon we shall walk o'er the hills of bright glo-ry,

O say, will you go to the E-den a-bove?
O say, will you go to the E-den a-bove?
O say, will you go to the E-den a-bove?
And drink the pure joys of the E-den a-bove

Where we'll weary nevermore.

S. W. T.

1. There is rest beyond the stream, Where the lights celestial gleam,
2. Soon up-on the shining strand, We will hear the an-gel band,
3. Oh! how sweet 'twill be to meet, Where our bliss will be complete;

And we're pressing for the shore, Where we'll weary nev-er-more.
Singing "home, sweet home" at last Where the toil of earth is past.
Ev - er - more to dwell in love, Round the Father's throne above.

REFRAIN.

There we'll wea-ry nev-er-more, There we'll weary nev-er-more;
    wea - ry   wea - ry

We are pressing for the shore, There we'll weary nev - er-more.

114. Time is bearing us on.

1. Time is bear-ing us on to our heav-en-ly home,
Where af-flic-tion and sickness can nev-er-more come;
There the fountains of health will un-ceas-ing-ly play,
And the wa-ters of life wash dis-eas-es a-way.

2. Time is bear-ing us on to our heav-en-ly home,
Where no storm-beat-en bil-lows can throw up their foam;
But the beau-ti-ful tints of the a-zure blue sky,
Are a feast for the soul and de-light for the eye.

3. Just a lit-tle while longer and we will be there,
With the glo-ry-fied an-gels, white gar-ments to wear;
Thro' the land of the blest and the world of the free,
Ev-er on-ward and upward our jour-ney will be.

Ascended.

115

MISS M. T. SHELHAMAR.

1. One more loved one gone before us, Gone to make our path-way straight,
2. One more star in heaven is gleaming. Sheding forth a gold-en ray
3. Angels called her from the mortal—Called her from its sin and strife;

Stretching thro' the gloomy valley To the gleaming pearl-y gate;
O'er the path of loved ones toiling Up life's rug-ged wea-ry way;
From the death of living sorrow To the joys of end-less life;

One more sainted life transplanted To the garden of our Lord,
One more jewel in the kingdom Placed by Him who reigns a-bove,
Angels whispered, "Come up higher" As they led her heav-en'ly flight,

One more angel joins the chorus, Chanting songs of sweet ac-cord.
In the precious royal setting, Of his pure and per-fect love.
Up the shining spiral stairway, To the land of per-fect light.

The by-and-by.

Passing the veil.

MRS. C. L. SHACKLOCK.

1. On-ly a step in the dark-ness, Guid-ed by in-fi-nate love,
Pass-ing the veil that di-vid-eth Earth from the glo-ry a-bove.
Los-ing the care and the sor-row, Los-ing the turmoil and strife;
Gaining a peace never fail-ing Won in the bat-tle of life.

2. And in the regions im-mor-tal, In the bright mansions above,
Thro' all e-ter-ni-ty claim-ing All that is sa-cred to love.
In the pure light of the king-dom, Brighter than jewels can shine;
Eve-ry fond tie thou hast cherished; Love is for-ev-er di-vine.

Index.

Angel Care	6
A little while longer	36
Angel Visitants	24
Angel Friends	41
Almost Home	59
And He will make it plain	87
A Fragment	84
A day's march nearer home	102
Ascended	115
Beautiful angels are waiting	8
Bethany	26
Beautiful City	32
Beautiful Land	45
Bliss	107
Beyond the mortal	80
By love we arise	61
Come up thither	22
Come, gentle spirits	13
Consolation	93
Come, go with me	99
Day by day	58
Don't ask me to tarry	48
Evergreen shore	29
Evergreen side	69
Fold us in your arms	103
Fraternity	86
Flowers in heaven	53
Gathered Home	20
Gone before	31
Gentle words	43
Gratitude	63
Golden shore	91
Gathered home beyond the sea	83
Home of rest	30
He's gone	92
Here and there	66
I shall know his angel name	4
I'm called to the better land	72-73
I long to be there	76
Looking over	18
Looking beyond	9
Longing for home	12
Let men love one another	16
Live for an object	91
My arbor of love	14
My home beyond the river	44
Moving Homeward	21
My home is not here	109
My guardian Angel	79
Not yet	10
No weeping there	3
No death	88
Not yet for me	95
Never lost	106
Only waiting	27
Over there	47
One woe is past	106
Outside	64
Over the river I'm going	43
O bear me away	90
One by one	65
Passed on	98
Passing away	101
Parting Hymn	107
Passing the veil	119
Repose	16
Ready to go	54
Shall we know each other there	40
Sweet hour of prayer	17
Sweet meeting there	42
Sweet reflections	38
Sow in the morn thy seed	46
Star of truth	88
Silent help	92
She has crossed the river	100
Summer days are coming	105
They'll welcome us home	7
There's a land of fadeless beauty	23
They're calling us over the sea	35
Tenting nearer home	28
Trust in God	41
The land of rest	52
The Sabbath morn	64
The cry of the spirit	60
The silent city	67
The river of time	82
The angels are coming	85
The Lyceum	94
They are coming	96
The happy time to come	56
The happy by and by	68
The other side	78
The Eden of bliss	62
The region of light	74
The shining shore	81
The harvest	75
Time is bearing us on	114
The happy spirit land	112
The by-and-by	116
The Eden above	111
The angel ferry	118
Voices from the better land	37
We shall meet on the bright, &c	5
Welcome angels	13
Waiting 'mid the shadows	11
When shall we meet again	25
We welcome them here	33
We'll meet them by and by	51
Where shadows fall not, &c	55
We'll anchor in the harbor	57
We'll gather at the portal	70
We shall know each other there	89
We'll dwell beyond them all	97
Waiting to go	104
Waiting on this shore	110
We're journeying on	60
What must it be to be there	71
Where we'll weary nevermore	113
Whisper us of spirit life	117
Waiting at the river	108

CHANTS.

Come to me	18
How long	19
I have reared a castle often	39
Invocation chant	15

A. B. Kidder & Son's Music Typography.

www.ingramcontent.com/pod-product-compliance
Lightning Source LLC
Chambersburg PA
CBHW020128170426
43199CB00009B/687